LEADING FROM THE IN-BETWEEN

Crossing Bridges with Emerging Leaders

By John McAuley
with Brenda Melles

ENDORSEMENTS

In this important and wise book, *Leading from the In-Between*, John McAuley provides an expert, tested answer to the question "What explicit and heart-filled path can best prepare emerging leaders to succeed with the challenges and opportunities that lie before them?" This book is a must-read for anyone committed to leadership development.

MARILEE ADAMS, PHD
Author of *Change Your Questions, Change Your Life* and
Teaching that Changes Lives

To be an effective mentor to young emerging leaders today, *Leading from the In-Between* is a must-read. John truly lives what he teaches, and his passion to share his leadership experiences comes from a humble heart of a godly leader you can trust.

BO BOSHERS
President of Lead222

In *Leading from the In-Between*, John McAuley shares practical insights from years of experience. This book "from the trenches" for others "in the trenches" will make you a better leader and a more effective developer of other leaders.

STEVE MOORE
President of Missio Nexus

I love this book and fully agree with John's key message, the need to develop leaders with both character (EQ) and competence (IQ). Specializing with Gen Y in the workforce for both non-profit and Fortune 500 companies, I've seen first-hand the importance of developing both of these vital areas (IQ & EQ) as we encourage tomorrow's leaders. John also makes a keen observation on the power of mentoring in this process, as we have never seen mentoring play such a key role for leaders as in this century, where young people are increasingly turning to their workplace as their new "extended family." Thought-provoking and relevant, with much needed wisdom—I highly recommend this book!

DR. KARYN GORDON
Parenting/Gen Y Expert

Business and leadership books are their own industry these days. But John McAuley's contribution to the genre is an important addition. In the first place, John's life experiences are unique and significant to the topic. Secondly, leadership skills for young people have never been so important and needed. This is a must-read for those interested in the next generation and those who want to see how adversity can be overcome for the betterment of all.

TONY CLEMENT
Member of Parliament, Parry Sound-Muskoka

Defining leadership is a lot like trying to catch the wind. We see the trees swaying. We experience how the wind feels, but it is still elusive. *Leading from the In-Between* captures the elusive dynamics of leadership. The conceptual triads that frame John McAuley's leadership vision are grounded in what really happens at Muskoka Woods. Implementing the recommended leadership practices will keep you from being blown off course.

DON POSTERSKI
Author and Cultural Analyst

LEADING FROM THE IN-BETWEEN

Crossing Bridges with
Emerging Leaders

John McAuley
with Brenda Melles

CASTLE QUAY BOOKS

LEADING FROM THE IN-BETWEEN:
CROSSING BRIDGES WITH EMERGING LEADERS
Copyright © 2015 John McAuley
All rights reserved
Printed in Canada
International Standard Book Number: 978-1-927355-56-5 soft cover
E-book ISBN: 978-1-927355-57-2 EPUB
(E-book available from the Kindle Store, KOBO and the iBooks Store)

Published by:
Castle Quay Books
19-24 Laguna Pkwy, Lagoon City, Brechin, Ontario, L0K 1B0
Tel: (416) 573-3249
E-mail: info@castlequaybooks.com   www.castlequaybooks.com

Edited by Marina Hofman Willard, and Lori Mackay
Cover design by Clear Space Design & Communications Inc. and Burst Impressions
Printed at Essence Printing, Belleville, Ontario

Library and Archives Canada Cataloguing in Publication

McAuley, John, 1964-, author

    Leading from the in-between : crossing bridges with emerging leaders
/by John McAuley ; contributions by
Brenda Melles ; foreword by Phil Geldart.

Issued in print and electronic formats.
ISBN 978-1-927355-56-5 (pbk.).--ISBN 978-1-927355-57-2 (epub)

    1. Leadership. I. Melles, Brenda, author II. Title.

HD57.7.M317 2015   658.4'092   C2015-900646-5
                                       C2015-900647-3

CASTLE QUAY BOOKS

DEDICATION

To my parents—Edward and Myrtle McAuley
And to Muskoka Woods founders—Jack and Marie Boddy
I lead today because you are my bridge to "life to the full."
To Lori, Kasi and Jake
You are the daily inspiration that shapes my world.

TABLE OF CONTENTS

SECTION I—LEADING FROM THE IN-BETWEEN

    Key messages: Growing up in the in-between
                   What is this book about?
                   Building the right substructure
                   The end goal of leadership development for emerging leaders

SECTION II—FORMING THE RIGHT FOOTINGS— SHAPING YOUNG LEADERS WITH CHARACTER, COMPETENCE AND CADENCE

    Key messages: Shaping whole-person character in emerging leaders
                   Practicing affirmation
                   Embracing authenticity
                   Cultivating attunement
                   Character is not perfection

SECTION III—SPANNING THE DISTANCE—
MAXIMIZING INFLUENCE WITH EMERGING LEADERS

SECTION IV—TRANSVERSING TOGETHER—
POSITIONING EMERGING LEADERS
FOR EXCEPTIONAL DEVELOPMENT

FOREWORD

The oaks of the future lie in today's acorns. Accordingly, nurture and care provided in the present is crucial to ensuring healthy and mature growth in the years to come.

In *Leading from the In-Between*, John draws on his many years of working with emerging leaders. When built into the lives of younger leaders, the mindset and skills he shares nurtures them into strong, well-rooted "oaks."

John's experience with younger leaders and others seasoned in leadership is captured in these pages. His insight is a roadmap to success that avoids pitfalls and celebrates the prizes to be won.

The depth of John's understanding is clearly in evidence throughout the book. He creatively explains the viewpoints of those being served and illustrates how to equip future leaders for their maximum impact and success.

John's faith story is part of the weaving that underscores the importance of each individual's relationship with God. The idea of "cadence," which invites emerging leaders to "be in step with God," is refreshing.

The book is enriched by John's leadership experiences at Muskoka Woods. His passion for developing emerging leaders into all their potential inspires the rest of us to do the same.

PHIL GELDART
President/CEO, Eagles Flight

AUTHOR'S NOTE

When a band releases an album, you can be sure that many people have contributed to each track. There are songwriters, session musicians, singers, engineers and producers. Yet, when authors release a book, we often imagine they have sat in isolation in a room with a laptop and written every word and then pressed print.

This book was put together like a music album. The content was born out of my two decades of experience with emerging leaders, as the president and CEO of a large youth organization, and as a leader in the camping industry as a Christian minister. The content also springs from my graduate studies and teaching in leadership development over the past several years. I recognized early in this process that sitting alone with a blank screen and trying to write my thoughts on leadership was not going to work. Instead, I pulled together a team of people to bring this project together.

Brenda Melles played the most important role. I talked out my thoughts to her in many hours of interviews and phone conversations. She helped me organize and write my stack of stories in a way that could work for a reader. I invited other youth leadership development practitioners to participate in focus groups on some of the key content. I sat with writers who helped me organize the material. In the end, we wrote this book, which I hope reads like a great playlist, each chapter a fresh melody that echoes what is before and crests toward what is next.

In 2010, with the help of Ellen and Tim Duffield and Dave Garda, I published a napkin sketch model of leadership development in a small fieldbook called *Leader to Leadership*. This book expands that basic framework and puts flesh on the bones of what were simple graphics and short phrases. I'm indebted to Emily Duffield, Kathlene Evans and Rachel Thiessen, who spent time and energy sharpening the Leader to Leadership Model, which contributed to the clarity of this book.

Everything I am as a leader, earthly speaking, is made possible because of my family. Lori, you are the reason I am able to daily stand firm; you are the most gracious leader I know. Kasi, your incredible creativity reminds me every day to look deeper at our world and do something about it. Jake, your bold loyalty and positive presence remind me every day to believe the best in all. My love for the three of you is my most important leadership work.

I first saw leadership embodied in my own home. My mum and dad surrounded themselves with young emerging leaders; all else is measured by their godly example and love. I continue to be energized by the lives of Nana and Poppa Boddy. Their vision and generosity inspire us all to believe we can "shape our world." One day, we truly hope and pray we can see their vision become a reality—to raise up a future prime minister.

To all the Muskoka Woods staff and family, you have patiently endured my leadership, including those best-self and not-so-best-self moments. I pray I will live up to all this book seeks to affirm.

I am a better leader today because of a rich cluster of mentors, past and present. Thank you for creating both the space and the personal encouragement to stretch my wings and fly.

To Bono, The Edge, Larry and Adam: your life and music inspired me as a teen growing up in Northern Ireland. Bono, you are the impetus of the leadership definition I wrote and seek to inspire others toward each day: "Leaders are people who look at their world and say 'It doesn't have to be this way' and do something about it."

PREFACE

Each week, five new books on leadership hit the market.

As one writer said, "We may be out of trees before we understand leadership."

This book is my contribution.

Leadership is situational. The dynamics of leadership cannot be reduced to a rigid formula. Sometimes, more experienced leaders are in front, paving the way. In other situations, they are walking alongside. And then there are occasions when they lead from below. The more experienced leader surrenders to the less experienced and invites them to "stand on my shoulders."

My preference is to multi-image leadership dynamics as bridges. When working with emerging leaders, we can be the bridge. We can bridge what is with what can be. Other situations require us to be bridge builders. The challenge is to span the distance of "the in-between." Whatever the distance, the objective is to get over the bridge together. The best way to think about the frameworks that comprise this book is to envision us crossing bridges with emerging leaders.

Like the basic model, this book is structured around three triads. The first triad is cadence, character and competence. These are the footings we need to form in emerging leaders to anchor their ongoing leadership development. The second triad is mentors, coaches and sages. These are the three roles that, especially woven together, accompany and inspire young people toward a life of exceptional leadership. The final triad is see, stretch and support. These are the strategies we use to help emerging leaders traverse the distance between the reality of their world now and the preferred future they want to build.

This book is full of real-life stories that express and amplify other theories and research about leadership development for emerging leaders. Some stories come from my early roots, and others are from the more recent past. My leadership model was birthed and operationalized with young people at Muskoka Woods, and much of what I have learned comes from there. Scattered throughout this book are quotes from young people who have participated in Muskoka Woods' CEO leadership development program. These quotes are from interviews of participants in this program by my colleague Chris Tompkins for his master's degree research.[1] The stories and quotes help remind us that this book is more about practice than theory. Leadership development plays out in the real lives of real young people, and effective leadership development experiences have to have real consequences. The stories bring those to light.

All of us operate from a worldview that shapes who we are, and mine is framed by my Christian faith. The Psalms—that beautiful set of biblical poetry of wisdom, confession, lament, thanksgiving and praise—have sustained my leadership over the years. They have given me permission as a leader to say, I'm afraid, I don't have the answers and I need help. Phil Geldart, founder and chief executive officer of Eagle's Flight, is one of my most important mentors and has spent hundreds of hours with me, helping me shape my view of leadership development. Early on in our relationship, Phil introduced me to Psalm 78:70–72, which says, "He chose David his servant…and David shepherded them with integrity of heart; [and] with skillful hands." That verse, which weaves around the ideas of character, competence and cadence, helped me uncover this leadership model.

I find immense inspiration in the lives of great leaders, but none more than Jesus. Each day I ask myself, am I allowing the beauty and character of Jesus to be reflected in my life and my leadership? After all, who doesn't want life to the full, where love, joy, peace, kindness and gentleness reign? I am convinced that life is not an accident. We are all created and loved by God. I believe that the best of life happens when we are a living exhibition of life with God.

My worldview is reflected in this book, but I hope I have expressed it in a way that opens up conversation and connection rather than closing it down. My favourite and most stimulating conversations are usually with people who see life differently than I do.

Finally, I read very widely on leadership, management and youth development. I am sometimes unaware of when other people's words have become mine. I have tried my best in this book to give credit to the people who have

---

[1] For the purpose of anonymity all the names have been changed.

shaped my ideas. However, if you see something and recognize its source, please send me an email so I can ensure that the people are acknowledged rightly for their work.

This book is written for people who are pouring their lives and energy into emerging leaders, that fascinating group of young men and women who are living in an in-between stage of life, ripe for growth, learning and inspiration. In a world of leadership books, my hope is that this one not only affirms what you know but also gifts you with something new you haven't yet discovered.

John McAuley
john@theleadershipstudio.ca

Section I

LEADING FROM THE IN-BETWEEN

Chapter 1

BE THE BRIDGE

GROWING UP IN THE IN-BETWEEN

I was born in Northern Ireland in 1964 and spent my childhood, youth and early adulthood in Belfast. The early sixties marked the beginning of more than three decades of intense and violent conflict in my hometown. This period is called "The Troubles," and troubling it was. Northern Ireland was an unwelcome place. We used to tell the joke of a man from India who first gets off the plane in Belfast and is asked, "What's your religion?" The man responds, "I'm Hindu." And the Irish interrogator fires back, "Are you a Catholic Hindu or a Protestant Hindu?"

That was the world of Northern Ireland. It was an environment of Us and Them. Catholics and Protestants. Loyalists and Republicans. Wealthy and poor. Right side and wrong side. There were sharp lines about acceptable beliefs and behaviours, especially in the Church. Some were in. Some were out. No grey.

I grew up in a Protestant church right on the front lines of it all. The church hall was literally on the Protestant side of the neighbourhood, and the sanctuary was in a

KEY MESSAGES

- Leaders look at their world and say "It doesn't have to be this way" and do something about it.
- The greatest leverage for leadership lies in the "in-between" places.
- Mentors, coaches and sages develop emerging leaders with character, competence and cadence by seeing, stretching and supporting them.

23

Catholic IRA-controlled stronghold. Our services were guarded by a dozen soldiers. Most of the neighbourhood residents were hard-working shipyard factory families. Many of the fathers were absent. Drinking and abuse were common. Young people were easily drawn into the Troubles, and some were tangled up with paramilitary forces. When I was 18, my friend Karen McKeon, an innocent and much respected member of our church, was tragically murdered on the church doorstep in an act of political violence. Her life and her death had a tremendous shaping influence on our church and on me personally.

That polarization of Us and Them was my world, but somehow my family lived in the "in-between." They seemed to be able to see across the barriers and even bridge between them. In my house, bigotry was not allowed, and anti-Catholicism was off limits. In the midst of our fractured and working class community, I lived in a comfortable upper-middle-class home with two loving and supportive parents. We were Protestants, but one of my mother's best friends was a Catholic, and I had a real crush on a young Catholic woman. At that time, churches had rules about things like drinking and smoking and were legalistic, and people were defined by what they did and didn't do. But my family wasn't imprisoned by that and seemed to find a way to accept people no matter what side of the line they fell on. We vacationed in the Republic, the south of Ireland, despite the fact it was judged by many to be feeding the enemy. In subtle ways and in direct ways, my family shaped me to be an embracing person. I grew up encouraged to live in the in-between.

At age 18, I joined the Royal Ulster Constabulary, and I spent four and a half years working as a police officer. For long hours, I would ride in the small space in the back of a police wagon with three other officers. Our lives, literally, depended on each other. Bessbrook station, where I was first assigned, had the unenviable reputation of being the police station that had lost the most officers to death. We were paid to enact justice, mercy and grace—and every day, we would have to make judgments on what that would look like. I quickly realized that many of those decisions were not as black and white as we had so long been told. My culture schooled me on the Protestant versus Catholic divide. But the first time I was shot at, it was in a Protestant stronghold. There may be no quicker way to lose the conviction that one side is always right and one side is always wrong than the sound of a bullet aimed in your direction.

At age 21, in the midst of my life as a police officer, I had a dramatic experience with God. I turned my back on the self-destructive patterns and partying lifestyle I had developed to deal with the stress, anxiety and trauma of my work.

Then, for 18 more months, I sat in that same police wagon with the same guys. They were the same, the outside world was the same, yet I was radically changed. Living my new life as a genuine and authentic apprentice of Jesus in the back of that police wagon remains one of the greatest challenges I have faced as a Christian.

These are the stories of my roots. These are the stories that have shaped me as a person, as a Christian and as a leader. I remember as a child feeling that I never really belonged. I often felt judged because I didn't quite fit. I was in the in-between. I was a Protestant who went to church in a Catholic part of town. I was upper middle class in a struggling neighbourhood. I was a Christian in a police truck. I grew up in a social environment that was sharp and polarized. But I never was able to understand how you could hate people so much when actually you had so much in common. Not then, and never since, have I ever been able to comfortably live in a world of Us and Them.

I am glad my life story starts in the Emerald Isle. Some of the greatest leaders in the world have their roots there. Bono, my favourite of the batch, sings at the end of the song *Sunday Bloody Sunday*, "No more! No more!" We don't have to live this way. There is a better way, and we can get there. It is leadership that moves people toward a preferred future and away from an unwanted current reality. Leadership is the core practice that accompanies change. Change requires leaders, and leaders navigate change.

Up from the roots of my life, inspired by Bono's "No more!" cry, shaped by my apprenticeship with Jesus and influenced by the words and thinking of so many others, here is how I define leadership:

Leaders are people who look at the world and say "It doesn't have to be this way" and do something about it.

My story started in Northern Ireland, but it doesn't end there. For the past two decades, my life has been in Canada. I work as president and CEO of Muskoka Woods, a Christian youth resort. I've moved across the ocean, but I still live and work in the in-between. Canadians are known the world over for being peacemakers and intermediaries, bridging the distance between conflict and calm, and modeling a peaceful society of multiculturalism and diversity. That's the cultural ethos I am proud to live in.

I work with young people—those who are in an in-between stage of life, neither children nor mature adults. About 25,000 of them, primarily aged 7 to 25, come through Muskoka Woods each year. We train another 350 staff members to live out our mission, "inspiring youth to shape their world." That is the group of young people I aspire to influence.

Although I am a Christian minister by training and vocation, I spend much of my time in sparkling conversation with young people and other leaders who do not share my faith, creating space for connection and experiences that bring us together.

My role is to be a leader, and these in-between spaces are where I thrive. I know what it is to live in a context of conflict and judgment. But I am comfortable in the tension. I am not afraid of ambiguity and mystery. I thrive in a diverse place. I believe I am called to be a bridge builder, to bring people together, to create space. I'm wired in my spirit to see the best in people, to not judge people on what they believe and to exercise patience with people who would normally get written off. I was knit together in a context of complexity. I was formed in the in-between—and I believe that the in-between is where the greatest leverage for leadership lies.

The Muskoka Woods Leadership Studio is one of my favourite places to be—not just because of the beautiful weathered timber and the incredible design of the physical space, but also as a metaphor for leadership development. Getting to the front door and into the studio requires you to traverse a 210-foot suspension bridge that spans the gap between regular camp life and the studio.

We built the bridge because we were inspired by a medieval Welsh myth about the good king Llyr. Llyr is a man of immense proportions, as big as a mountain. His daughter, the beloved maiden Branwen, is promised in marriage to the king of Ireland. But when she moves across the sea, she is badly mistreated. When word gets back to Wales of the punishment and disgrace that have befallen her, the Welsh king Llyr is enraged. A host of ships sail to Ireland to rescue her, with Llyr wading alongside them because no ship can contain him. When the Irish see them coming, they burn the bridge over the river so that no man or ship can cross. Arriving at the river's bank, the Welsh nobles ask their giant king for counsel. Llyr says, *"A fo ben, bid bont"*—"The one who will be a leader must also be a bridge." Then Llyr lays his body across the river, and his men walk across his back to the other side.

The leader is the bridge across the in-between. The bridge between the now and the not yet, the bridge between the current reality and the preferred future, the bridge who inspires change. The bridge is my dominant metaphor for my identity as a leader. I can look across the span to see where something needs to happen and then be the bridge.

WHAT IS THIS BOOK ABOUT?

THIS BOOK IS ABOUT LEADERSHIP, BUT PERHAPS NOT THE LEADERSHIP YOU THINK YOU KNOW.

When I did my first course in the Master of Organizational Leadership program at Cairn University in Philadelphia, the chair of the program, Dr. Jay Desko, put six words up on the whiteboard: strong, visionary, successful—and chaos, confusion and complexity.

The dominant expectation of leaders today is that they must be strong, visionary and successful. Much of the thinking and literature on leadership development is centred on creating these qualities. We expect our leaders to be heroes, their capes trailing in the wind behind them. We expect them to hold within them all the right answers. And as a result, many leaders live with horrendous pressure to operate in a way that makes them appear to fit the part.

However, the daily realities of leadership are not strength, vision and success. They are chaos, confusion and complexity—and it is these qualities for which we must equip our leaders. This has probably never been truer than it is right now, when the pace of change in our world is unparalleled. We need to let go of the caricature of the strong, successful visionary leader and instead embrace the image of leaders who humbly and authentically know who they are, who mobilize the collective strengths of those around them and who excel at navigating systems and diversity. We need leaders who can work in the in-between and be the bridge to positive change.

I was doing a spiritual formation exercise with Muskoka Woods senior staff, most of them in their late teens or early twenties. As we walked, we came across an old tire that had washed up on the beach. I stood there praying, discovering in this tire a great vehicle for me to talk with God. I picked it up and carried it back toward our meeting room to use as an illustration. On the way, various people tried to take it from my hands and throw it out, but I said, "No. I realize that I feel like this tire. I'm worn out, bald from running on the road for a long time. I know that if I don't tend to some dangers, I will have a blowout." People in the room were surprised by my vulnerability.

Often, a leader's followers want him or her to be a strong, visionary, perfect picture. But, instead of an illusion of perfection, you want a leader who humbly understands what she or he is not. When all leaders say is "I'm fired up and strong," there is no room for growth in their lives. Much of the leader's life is coming to the end of ourselves and saying "I need others." Effective leaders know how to gather around them what they need to move themselves or their team or their enterprise in the right direction.

THIS BOOK ADDRESSES LEADERSHIP IN ALL THREE SPHERES— SELF, TEAM AND ORGANIZATION.

Over time, people have asked me, "Why do you spend so much time thinking about and reading about leadership? Not everyone is a leader, and not everyone needs to cultivate the core practice of leadership." I disagree—at least in part— because leadership operates on three levels.

The first is the sphere of leading self. In this sphere, none of us are excused. We lead to live. Without taking on the mantle of leadership, how can you lead yourself out of bed each morning into purposeful action? If you cannot lead yourself, you are powerless to respond to the change that comes at you in your everyday life and live into your preferred future.

The second is the sphere of team leadership. While we all lead at the level of self, a smaller but substantial subset of us also leads others. Team leadership may show up in the classroom, on the schoolyard, in the workplace, at camp or in a church or other place of worship. No matter how skilled, how gifted, how competent, no one person is entirely sufficient for all situations. That's where team leadership comes into play.

The third is the sphere of organizational leadership. You know you are in this sphere when the purpose of your leadership serves someone else who is expecting value. When I try to get on a hockey team, it's about personal leadership—my own skill, drive and discipline are what help me reach my goal. When I'm the captain of the team, it's about team leadership—we train and play together with the goal of winning our games. But when I am the general manager of Team Canada, it's about enterprise leadership—because our team's purpose is much bigger than just winning a game. We also carry the hopes of the fans and the nation, alongside pleasing sponsors and meeting expectations.

If you struggle with leading self, you will struggle with leading others. And if you struggle with leading others, you will struggle with leading an enterprise. This book tackles the challenges of leadership in all three spheres.

THIS BOOK IS ABOUT EMERGING LEADERS.

Born in the late 1980s or early 1990s, emerging leaders live in a different world than the one I grew up in and face challenges I never had to address.

28

Today's young people live in a world marked by more accelerated change than at any other moment in human history. Many of them will grow up to work in jobs that have not yet been invented, using technology we cannot yet imagine. The list of acceptable options for their lifestyle choices, family models, education, religious expressions and moral practices is more expansive than it has ever been before. Their social, cultural and belief landscape is shifting sand.

We often speak as if young people have created the world in which they live. But the truth is, they have inherited it. Pluralism, relativism, consumerism, technological innovation, postmodernism—this is the only world they have ever known. As one of my mentors, Don Posterski, says, they have inherited in the micro what the older generation of adults have put in place in the macro.

These emerging leaders are the group of people I work with in my role as president and CEO of Muskoka Woods. The decade between age 16 and 26 can be a period of incredible leadership formation. Over the years, I have crossed paths with thousands of young people in this stage, and I have had the privilege of giving mentoring, coaching and spiritual direction to many. Along the way, I have seen that the nature of the world they live in creates particular strengths and challenges for them as leaders. In such a time as this, how do we develop emerging leaders?

This book aims to deepen understanding about where emerging leaders are at and what kind of world they live in. It aims to inspire and equip young people—and the coaches, mentors and sages that accompany them—to look at the world and say "It doesn't have to be this way" and do something about it.

FINALLY, THIS BOOK IS ABOUT LEADERSHIP DEVELOPMENT.

Venture capital investors step out on the edge and throw their weight behind ideas that are unproven and risky—but also carry the potential for being highly profitable. The art is seeking out these ideas in their early stages, before they are clearly valuable to the rest of the world. Venture capital investors invest not only in what things are but also in what they can become.

Leadership development is also a venture. It has both risk and reward. If we are convinced that leaders are strong, visionary and successful, that is who we will seek, and that is what we will equip people to become. Often it seems that people only want to invest in those who have "arrived."

When it comes to young people and to leadership development, I'm more interested in the people who are rough around the edges. All of us—you, me, any young person we ever encounter—are unfinished. Each of us are both being and becoming. Many emerging leaders are easily missed. Nurturing leaders is not automatic. Leadership development with emerging leaders takes a vision of who young people are and who they can become. It takes intention, and it takes great tools.

The heart of this book is a simple but powerful way to pursue leadership development with young people:

- SEE…emerging leaders for who they are and who they can become.
- STRETCH…emerging leaders to do and be more than they thought possible.
- SUPPORT…emerging leaders as they both succeed and fail.

To develop leaders that say *"It doesn't have to be this way" and do something about it*, you need a framework for change, a philosophy of understanding how people are transformed and how they develop. "See–stretch–support" is that overarching philosophy of leadership development. Whether you are talking about corporate leadership or spiritual formation, a framework to guide your strategy of leadership development is tremendously helpful. The see-stretch-support framework is echoed in other writing and thinking on leadership development. It builds on the wisdom of others and fits with our lived experience with emerging leaders.

BUILDING THE RIGHT SUBSTRUCTURE

I am not an engineer, but I have learned that there are two major components to bridge building. The first is the substructure. It includes all of the things that provide support to the bridge—the abutments, the footings, the pilings and so on. The second is the superstructure, which includes all of the things that span the river—the bridge deck, the parapets, the sidewalk and so on. The substructure is dug into the earth or bedrock below and is usually unseen. The superstructure is visible, even from afar.

When bridges do not have the right substructure in place in the early stages of construction, they eventually give way and fall down. The same is true of leadership development for emerging leaders. If a solid substructure is not in place, there is great risk of collapse.

There are three critical components to the substructure of leadership development for young people:

- CHARACTER—being honest and true
- COMPETENCE—doing the right things the right way
- CADENCE—sustaining leadership by keeping in step with yourself, others and God

30

I have seen far too many leaders who showed great promise and potential in their teens and 20s crumble, lose heart or burn out by their 30s and 40s. If you don't sort out the substructure at the beginning, you will deal with it later, sometimes at tremendous cost. It may be a collapse of character. It may be a failure of competence. Or it may be a crash of cadence. Either way, the substructure of leadership development, the footings, can and should be built in the early life of an emerging leader. This book aims to lay out why and how. The next chapters deepen each of these areas with key leadership development concepts, research and stories from real experience.

THE END GOAL OF LEADERSHIP DEVELOPMENT FOR EMERGING LEADERS

Leadership guru Stephen Covey famously wrote that leaders "begin with the end in mind." Leadership is always about ends, goals and results.

What is the end goal for leadership development with young people? That young people would look at their world and say "It doesn't have to be this way" and do something about it. They would be the bridge. Leadership is inextricably connected to change. Leadership begins with change, and leaders navigate change—by bridging the in-between, from the dissatisfied now to the preferred future.

What are the means to inspire and equip emerging leaders to shape their world? By building the substructure—cadence, character and competence.

This book is written for the mentors, coaches and sages who are pouring themselves into the next generation. You may be working with emerging leaders in the Christian context—in a church, youth organization or community program. Or you may be working with young people in other contexts—a school, community centre, club or team. Regardless of the in-between spaces in which you encounter young people, I believe you will find plenty of value here to carry into your work.

How can emerging leaders be the bridge? What are the critical issues for today's emerging leaders on character, competence and cadence? How do we see, stretch and support them? What specific strategies work for leadership development with young people? How do we inspire them to change their world? Read on.

Section II

FORMING THE RIGHT FOOTINGS

Shaping Young Leaders
with Character, Confidence
and Cadence

Chapter 2

CHARACTER

**Being Honest
and True**

SHAPING WHOLE-PERSON CHARACTER IN EMERGING LEADERS

KEY MESSAGES

- Character is bigger than morality—and is revealed in all our thoughts, feelings and behaviours.

- We shape character in emerging leaders by practicing affirmation, embracing authenticity and cultivating attunement.

- Character is not perfection—we are all unfinished.

Let me begin with a confession.

In 1988, during my first year of college, when the exam for my leadership and management course was scheduled, I arranged to write it early. I had already planned a trip home to Northern Ireland, so I couldn't be there for the scheduled exam date. My professor was accommodating. He led me into a resource room at the end of a corridor near his office. I sat at the table and put my briefcase beside me. He closed the door and wished me luck. As I wrote the exam, every now and again my professor would come in the room and check on me. All was going well until I got to a question about Blanchard and Hershey's situational leadership theory. As I filled out the chart on leadership styles, I began to doubt my answer and worry if I was mixing something up. The question was worth a big proportion of the exam mark, and I wanted to get it right. At the moment of my internal questioning, my professor came in to the room. I waited until he left, then quickly grabbed my briefcase, opened it up and checked my cards. When I confirmed that I had the right answer, I continued to write the exam.

That summer, I was speaking on integrity at Muskoka Woods. As I prepared for my talk, I prayed, "God, if there is anything in my life where I have not acted with integrity, please help me to see it."

Well, instantly about five things came to my mind. One of them was that I cheated on the leadership and management exam.

Not only that, in an unbelievable irony, the very same professor of the very same leadership and management course was coming to Muskoka Woods that week. There I was, about to speak on integrity, and who was to be in the audience but the professor of the class whose exam I cheated on. Only God has this sense of humour. I knew immediately that I needed to go speak to my professor before the event. I knew then as I know now that when I blow it on character, when I am not at my best, when I act without integrity, I need to go put it right.

I found him on the property and pulled him aside. I told him what happened and confessed that if I had written the answer wrong, I was going to change it. He said to me, "I appreciate you telling me that. I believe that you are acting with integrity; I'm confident you had it right anyway, and you don't need to worry about it." I was very thankful for his graciousness. In that moment, I was struck anew by the realization that being an effective leader does not mean you'd better get an A in your leadership course. Instead, I had a deep conviction that my character needs to be the determinant of my longevity and effectiveness as a leader.

Being a person of character is often directly correlated to your sphere of influence. If you are not a person of character, you may well climb the ladder to great heights. However, if you do not attend to the pieces of your broken character, there will come a time when you will meet with a catastrophic failure. The consequences for missteps in character are exponentially more powerful than for missteps in competence. They linger longer, and the wound is deeper. A life of hiddenness and deception is almost always revealed in the end. If you don't take character development seriously, you will severely limit your sphere of responsibility and influence.

What is character? Character is being honest and true, through and through, in my whole person. In ancient times, unscrupulous potters would sometimes cover over the cracks in their clay pots with wax to disguise the pot's imperfections. On the outside, the pot would look smooth and sound. But once you poured hot water into it, the wax would melt, and the pot would begin to leak. As a result, honest potters started labeling their pots "*sin cere*"—literally, "without wax."

When you bought a *sin cere* pot, you could be confident that the way the pot looked on the outside was a fair picture of its true character. A *sin cere* pot was made only with the earth's rich, dark clay, well-crafted and fired, through and through. Like the clay pot, the character we want is whole and complete, with integrity between what shows on the surface and what is hidden underneath.

Most of the conversations around character have been narrow in their scope. Character is often reduced to moralism and personal lifestyle choices. We focus on how well young people follow "the rules" of good behaviour. Instead of asking "What are you learning in your life?" "How are your friendships?" or "What are your hopes for what you will become?" we're more concerned with the old-school trio of sex, drugs and alcohol. In other words, we've often defined good character by what people *don't* do, rather than what they *do*. Whenever we do this, we reduce character to moralism—and we miss an opportunity to truly see young people for who they are.

We also reduce the fulsome meaning of character when we define it as who you are when you are alone, when no one else is looking. True, character is sometimes revealed behind closed doors and in the dark without the spotlight of public view. However, character is not only who I am when I am alone; it is also who I am when I am active in the outside world with my friends and strangers looking on. One of the greatest challenges for young people in this generation is to find that match between who I am when I am alone and who I am when I am active and on show in the world. Because the value of acceptance reigns so supreme in the ethos of today's young people, they typically have little problem "giving permission" to others to be who they are and behave as they will. However, for a young person to "take permission" to be who I am and behave as I believe is right, especially if it is in contradiction to others around me, is far more challenging. Emerging leaders are likely to disguise their real selves for the sake of letting their audience hear what they want to hear, rather than what they need to hear. In the age of acceptance, for a young person to stand up and say "This is right" and "You are wrong" is social suicide. Developing character means facing questions like not only "Who am I when I am alone?" but also "Who am I when I'm in front of people?" "What am I when I am not in a leadership position?" and also "Who am I as a leader in front of people whose opinion I care about?"

In summary, character is much wider and deeper than morality and lifestyle. And it is much bigger than who I am when I am alone. Character is connected to the integrity of the whole person and the motives of the heart.

Fundamentally, character is all of who I am, with all my strengths and skills, active and on show in my life in private and public. Like the *sin cere* pot, character is who I am as a whole person, through and through.

> *"A leader with good character is definitely someone who acts with honesty. You cannot, under any circumstances, compromise your morals and your beliefs. No matter if you're in a game situation or a life situation, compromising, lying, stealing and cheating are never OK. Because character is such a big component to being an effective leader. Because, if people can't trust you in a game-like situation, then how can you expect them to trust you in real life?"*—**JILLIAN**

Each of us has our own unique constellation of character. Martin Siegelman is the director of the Positive Psychology Center at the University of Pennsylvania and the founder of positive psychology. Siegelman's research explores and measures concepts like well-being, happiness and character strengths, which may include things like curiosity and interest in the world, forgiveness and mercy, bravery and valour. A person's top character strengths are called "signature strengths."

I agree with the positive psychologists. I believe that there are certain identifiable qualities about the way we are wired, about the way we are knit together in the womb, about our unique character. We can identify them—and even, if we are scientists, measure them. They are part of who we are, part of how God has made us. Character shows up in our thoughts, feelings and behaviours. And when we consider developing character in emerging leaders, we need to see their whole person, all their thinking, being and doing, and help them understand how they can bring their signature strengths to every situation.

Recently, I sat in a room with a young leader in my role as a leadership coach. In our conversation, it became more and more clear that even though it was just he and I sitting around the table, there was in fact something else in the room—his inner critic, or what I call "the nagging voice." This young man's nagging voice was moving him to self-criticism and giving him a sense of total lack of empowerment to address the challenge he was facing.

That was the moment to draw on one of his signature strengths—in his case, the strength of gratitude. I said to him, "One of the things I really appreciate about you is your sense of gratitude. In the circumstance you're in, is there anything about it that you can be grateful for?" Immediately, energy returned to the conversation. Encouraging one of his signature strengths lifted him out of the pit almost immediately. With encouragement through a signature strength, he was able to be lifted out of the pit almost immediately.

I am created, wired, to have character. Many of my strengths are rooted in my character. Yet, when I am overshadowed by my inner critic or fears, these strengths lie dormant. My character is made up of all that is within me—not only what I don't do but what I do; not only my brokenness but my signature strengths. As leaders, character is about living into all that we are and fulfilling what we are called to do.

Character development has long been a central goal of youth development. This may be because of the increasing research that links certain strengths of character to positive outcomes, like school success and helping others, and away from problem behaviours, like violence and drug and alcohol abuse.[2] But more often, our emphasis on character development is probably rooted in a basic feeling that good character is a good thing—it helps young people thrive, and it is how we are designed to live.

> *"Leaders with good character are conscious of the decisions they're making and the way they're impacting other people. In addition I'd say that good leaders with character wonder how the actual process of whatever they're doing is affecting the people who are planning it. So, not only how it's impacting the world, but if everybody's being included in the decision-making process, if everybody's voice is being heard. A leader with character cares more about how the job gets done than if the job gets done."*—**NATHAN**

But there's a problem, a crack in the pot. When it comes to living robust lives of character, we are all without full integrity. We are all unfinished and haunted by our own brokenness. We all have some wax mixed into our clay pot. How then do we go about developing character in emerging leaders? Here are three broad strategies for shaping character in emerging leaders:

- PRACTICING AFFIRMATION
- EMBRACING AUTHENTICITY
- CULTIVATING ATTUNEMENT

These practices operate in all three spheres of leadership—self, team and organization.

---

2 Nansook Park, "Character Strengths and Positive Youth Development," *The Annals of the American Academy of Political and Social Science* 591 (Jan. 2004): 40–54.

PRACTICING AFFIRMATION

Early in my career, I attended a large conference organized by a management association. After the conference, the organizers invited twelve young leaders to attend a small session with the conference's keynote speaker. I was selected to be part of this group. The speaker was Ken Blanchard, an author and management expert who had written over thirty books—many of which I had read, and some of which had sold millions of copies and been translated into dozens of languages. Let's be honest; I walked into the room intimidated and reserved. In fact, I felt again like an eight-year-old boy on the schoolyard, terrified of the older bullying boys, withdrawn and resigned. In two hours of the session with this small dynamic group, I made only one comment. I was so frightened of saying something wrong and looking foolish that I chose to withdraw and fade into the background. I had much to offer—not so much in terms of new models or ideas, but in terms of insightful questions and provocative comments. I was so ready to learn. But instead, I sat silent, paralyzed by fear.

In that moment, I needed great affirmation. At the first break, an older man who had played a role in selecting me to be a part of the group came over and said, "John, I've heard you've been silent in this room of twelve. Are you doing OK?" I responded by telling him how intimidated I felt in this company. This older man knew me. He spoke into me and affirmed me for who I was. As the session went on, it was that affirmation that freed me not only to listen but also to speak and participate—to show up.

Affirmation is fundamental to the character development of emerging leaders, particularly when leading self. It liberates people to be who they really are and become their best selves. The more confident emerging leaders are in who they are, the more likely it is that they will "show up" in the room and be the most effective leaders they can be.

There are many moments in my own life when I have chosen not to show up. Looking back on those times, I can see that the leaders who were attending to my development had not done the hard work of really getting to know me and my story, my brokenness and the wounded parts of me. Instead, they wrote me off. One of the effects of their not knowing and affirming my character was a list of missed opportunities for me to grow and develop as a leader.

Our leadership development with young people is often about giving them tasks and experiences to try out their leadership skills. However, a huge piece of our work is to take time to discover their character and their signature strengths. Our character-shaping efforts need to not only address what is broken and weak but also deepen that which is sound and true. If we truly see emerging leaders for who they are, we can then respond to them with affirmation in both their successes and failures. We need to affirm young people early for their being, not just their doing.

EMBRACING AUTHENTICITY

David Benner is a psychologist and spiritual director who wrote *The Gift of Being Yourself: The Sacred Call to Self-Discovery.* Benner begins with Augustine, the ancient theologian and philosopher who wrote "Oh God ever the same, let me know myself, let me know you." The premise is that you cannot know yourself without knowing God, and you cannot know God without knowing yourself. Benner writes of the lifelong process of knowing God and knowing yourself in an authentic way. He also highlights the serious dangers of avoiding self-discovery. Benner's insights have a major effect on the practices we use to shape character in emerging leaders. Not only do we need to practice affirmation, we also have to embrace authenticity. The key to authenticity is to know yourself—not just who you are but who you're not, not just your strengths but also your weaknesses.

One of our dominant cultural messages is the idea that you can be anything you want to be. Young people hear this message with regularity, through the movies they see, the slogans they read and the statements they are given by parents and other influential adults in their life. To be frank, I don't buy it.

I watched the early auditions for *American Idol* with my kids. A young woman came on the screen to sing. She was terrible—off tune, harsh, artificial. But after years of false affirmation from parents, coaches and teachers, she really believed she had exceptional talent. The *American Idol* judges cut off her song and began to criticize her painfully. When the audition was over, I asked our two kids, "If you were that bad, would you want me to pretend you were good?"

My teenage daughter turned to me and said, "Dad, if I sing that bad, please tell me."

Authenticity trumps pretense, every time. As people working with emerging leaders, we need to affirm them in who they are but make sure we allow them to become their authentic selves by helping them to discover who they are not. As we develop the character of emerging leaders, our work is to help them discover their authenticity and to help them recognize that they do not have to be everything and do everything. They can lead from their strengths while also recognizing their areas for growth. Even better, when leading in the team sphere, they can call upon the strengths of others in collaboration.

CULTIVATING ATTUNEMENT

Leaders can be affirmed at the level of self. They can be authentic, embracing their own strengths and weaknesses, and collaborative with a team of others. But faced with a reality that is marked by chaos, complexity and confusion, they can often fail to rise above that reality and bring their best self to the situation. Developing character in emerging leaders also means developing attunement—being keyed in to the reality at hand and knowing how to show up with your whole character so that you are part of the solution, not contributing to the problem.

When people describe the traits of good leaders, they usually use words like strong, visionary and successful. Leaders often experience tremendous pressure to do things that make them look just that way, even in the midst of incredibly difficult situations. We're often taught that leaders are supposed to be the people with all the answers. It takes incredible depth of character to say "I don't have the answer for this particular challenge right now, and the complexity of this is giving me huge pressure to perform in a way that might not be the most helpful."

> *"The leader needs to be able to lead the entire group, so stir up the entire group, get the whole group going and lead from afar. You can't get too sucked into the details, which is something that really stuck out to me."*—JAYDEN

Once young people move beyond leading small teams into leading more complex groups and enterprises, they are often confronted by complexity that unmoors them. When we are confused and under pressure, we often fall into the trap of overusing our strengths. One of my gifts as a leader is to be inspirational. But sometimes, inspiration is the last thing that is needed. Instead, leaders have to model an appropriate response that uses their strengths with the right tone to a given situation. When working with emerging leaders, early on we want to help them identify and work with complexities and tensions. Young people find this difficult and will often default to a "why bother?" response or to defeat. Emerging leaders tend to try to solve the tension before they even know what it is. Instead, we need to teach them to be much more attuned to who they are, the environment they are in and the tensions that live within them. Only with this attunement can we be sure that our best selves can show up.

An attuned leader is able to step back and ask, "What is going on in this environment? Where am I in this? What am I doing or not doing that is causing this to happen?" Ronald Heifetz and Marty Linsky write in *Leadership on the Line* that in the heat of leadership, leaders need to get off the dance floor and up on the balcony. There, separated from the noise and motion, they can discern patterns and get a better picture of what is going on.

CHARACTER IS NOT PERFECTION

Each summer, thousands of young people are interviewed to work at camps across North America. I looked at a set of interview questions for teenagers, and I was struck by their content on character. From the interview guide, you would think that we were trying to hire God, not young people! Too often with young leaders, we create language that makes life impossible for them to live up to. We create expectations that are unattainable for them. Most significantly, we nurture the idea that they are only right when they are perfect. But we are not perfect. None of us. This is not to say that we should not strive for excellence and depth of character development. But perfection talk does little more than cause young people to become overwhelmed and to run away and hide.

> *"If I was being led by someone I would want to know if what they were saying was true and if their intentions were honest. You can try to lead someone dishonestly, but in the longer term they'll find out, and you'll lose your reputation as a good leader."*—**CAROLINE**

I have a vivid memory from my teens of witnessing character triumph in the midst of imperfection. I was watching a badminton tournament. The atmosphere was intense and competitive, with some brilliant players on the court. In the midst of one game, the umpire made a series of miscalls. The tension grew, both on the court and at the sidelines. As the minutes ticked on, one of the players I deeply admired and respected as a leader finally reached his breaking point. He lost it, yelled at the umpire and stormed out of the gym, closing the door behind him. I thought to myself, *Oh wow, I can't believe he just did that.* But several minutes later, the same man walked back through the door into the gym. He waited until the game was over, came back on the court and walked to the umpire. He asked for a moment to address everyone and then apologized in the most profound and sincere way.

To this day, I am inspired by that moment. That leader provided a model for me that I have respected and tried to practice from then on. The reality is, leaders, even people of strong character, make mistakes—regularly—but the depth of their character drives the way they respond. The faster people are able to confess their shortcomings of character and work to make them right, the more depth of character they have. Character is often forged through adversity—but the way we react to adversity is so important. Can we model for emerging leaders how to put things right after we fail? Can we turn them toward confession? Can we take their challenges and make them a place of learning?

When it comes to character, we are all on a journey. We are all at various stages of growth, and we all have our own source of brokenness. The person of character is the person who is able to say "I am failing in this area, but I am ready to listen and to grow." The person of character is able to admit their mistakes, apologize and put things right. The person of character is the person who is able to say "I am unfinished, but I am open to being transformed."

Whether you are leading in the sphere of self, team or enterprise, character transcends every level and realm. Wherever you go, you take your whole self with you—not just what is on the surface but also all that is underneath, not just your strengths but also your imperfections. In the sphere of personal leadership, being genuinely affirmed helps develop a healthy self-confidence. In the sphere of team leadership, embracing authenticity liberates young leaders to not have to do everything but instead to call out the gifts and strengths of others. And in the sphere of enterprise leadership, being attuned to the current reality means that leaders can be creative, resourceful and courageous in the midst of complexity.

Character development starts early, and it needs to. Early in a young leader's life, taking shortcuts and cheating on issues of character may seem to have few consequences. But as a leader grows in position, influence and power, these bad character choices reverberate with severe consequences.

Leadership routinely gives you opportunities to abuse your position and authority. I remember hearing how the abuse of power starts innocently. We begin with "Wow, I get this? I am grateful." Without a careful watch on character, that attitude turns quickly to "I like this," then "I expect this," then "I deserve this," and finally, "I demand this." One of the clues that you are moving into abusive power is that your gratitude for your opportunities rapidly disappears. Instead, you begin to compare, to compete and to conspire. Shaping and nurturing the character of emerging leaders is critical for their healthy growth as people and for their effectiveness as leaders.

Chapter 3

COMPETENCE

Doing the Right Things the Right Way

BUILDING BASIC FOUNDATIONS OF COMPETENCE FOR EMERGING LEADERS

Every kid I grew up with played soccer—football, as it is called in most of the world—including me. George Best, the greatest footballer in the world, was a former student at my school. This was announced on day one. On the schoolyard, we were literally dribbling in the footsteps of giants. Our lives were set. We were all going to be famous footballers like George Best.

In truth, I was not even a half-decent footballer and could not compete in Mr. Best's company. In primary school, I was sure to make the team, but by the time I reached high school, the pool was much bigger. That was probably the first time I realized I wasn't as good at football as I thought I was. It didn't help that on the playground with me was Simon Fullerton, the best by far of all of us, an extraordinary young soccer player who could chip the ball right to my feet. Between the benchmarks of George Best and Simon Fullerton, it was hard not to lose heart.

KEY MESSAGES

- The best way to position emerging leaders for a lifetime of competence building is to begin with a small set of basic foundations.

- The major challenge of developing competence with emerging leaders is their lack of experience, which is the greatest teacher of competence.

- Choices, collaboration and complexity are at the roots of competency development.

45

The biggest fear of a kid on the sports field is of not getting picked or, perhaps worse, being picked last. So I decided I would become a goalkeeper, the position no one else wanted anyway. My first game, I let in 16 goals. But I did get better. The main reason for my improvement was that I hooked onto some of the science of goalkeeping, called "narrowing the angle." I learned that if you run out toward the players, the angle against which they can shoot the ball is radically changed. I picked up this lesson from reading a book on soccer skills written by George Best. When you stand between the posts, the opposing player can shoot up, down, left or right, and the keeper is left guessing. But if you narrow the angle, you can dramatically change your goalkeeping success. No matter what the shot, with that basic practice, my competence for keeping balls out of the net rose significantly.

Like character, competence is a central feature of most models of leadership development. Simply stated, competence is the ability to do the right things, the right way. When developing the competence of emerging leaders, we need to help them with a small set of basic foundations—things like narrowing the angle as a football goalkeeper. These basic foundations can vault their competence higher and serve them well across a wide variety of situations and tasks.

When I teach a course on leadership, one of my first exercises is to ask people to name the competencies and attributes of a leader. In a class of about 20 people, within 10 minutes we will have over a hundred competencies and attributes on the board. At that point I say, "That is God. That is not a leader."

Most conversations about leadership development and competence begin with list-making. To be an effective leader, people will say, you need to develop a certain list of behaviours or attributes. The list may include technical skill, emotional intelligence, effective communication, conflict resolution and so on. Much of the dialogue on competence is an argument about what is on the list. However, my view is that there is only one truly needed competence, and it is this: the competence of knowing which competence I need in this moment. When I am confronted with any leadership challenge, I ask three questions: What competence is needed? Who has it? And how do we bring it to bear in this situation? This is not to say that the competencies that make the "most important list" are not critical. For sure, a leader needs to demonstrate exceptional communication. However, knowing what the right kind of communication is, from whom, at the right time, is the true demonstration of competence.

When we are competent, we have the ability to use—or to identify and to find—the right knowledge, skills and capacity to do the things we are called to do, and to do them well.

The major challenge of developing competence with emerging leaders is their lack of experience—and experience is the greatest teacher and deepener of competence. Emerging leaders are often doing things they have, literally, never done before. They simply have not had the opportunities, built up over weeks, months and years, to test and sharpen their competence. They have not had the benefit of repeatedly applying their competence to complexity and chaos. Further, they have not accumulated the learning that comes from responding to failure.

I am often struck by the incredible ability of some of the young people I work with. On the surface, they appear highly competent. However, they lack the wisdom and resiliency that is built through experience. And it is the marriage between competence and wisdom that leads to great leadership results.

Ironically, the young people who wow us most with their gifts, skills and strengths may be the most vulnerable when it comes to leadership development. Why? Because there is a great danger of overestimating their competence and then demanding from them what is beyond their ability and reach. When their surface competence is unmoored from wisdom and experience, we can ask too much of them and set them up for failure. Over-confidence in their competence may be one of the most dangerous barriers to their learning.

There are no shortcuts to gaining the kind of wisdom that comes from weeks and years of experience. However, the best way to position emerging leaders for a lifetime of competence building is to help them "narrow the angle" and begin with a small set of basics. Rather than trying to make our way through a long list of competencies, a better strategy is to work with emerging leaders on a small set of foundations. When these foundations are strong, their impact will overflow to more specific competencies.

What makes up the foundation of competence? I want to emphasize three elements:

- SELF-KNOWLEDGE—to make mature choices
- COLLABORATION—to mobilize collective strengths
- COMPLEXITY—to navigate systems, culture and diversity

SELF-KNOWLEDGE—TO MAKE MATURE CHOICES

Just as self-discovery and embracing authenticity are such important elements in shaping the character of emerging leaders, so also is competence. "Know thyself" is ancient Greek wisdom that still resonates. To be competent you must know who you are—your signature strengths, your defaults, your brokenness, your self-talk. Self-awareness is essential for effective leadership, and not knowing yourself is a fatal flaw.

Not only must you know yourself, you must have the ability and readiness to change course. In other words, a leader needs the competence of both self-assessment and self-correction.

Leaders are often admired for jumping fearlessly into the fray, but just as often they need to step back and assess: What is really going on? Where am I in this? How do I need to show up in this situation? This is the same quality of attunement—getting off the dance floor and up onto the balcony—that is also at the heart of shaping character. If I do not know myself very well, my dramatic arrival on the scene may well be more negative than positive. Emerging leaders tend to leap from an idea right into action. Instead, they need to have the ability to stop themselves, self-assess and self-correct. When we built the Leadership Studio at Muskoka Woods, we designed this idea of self-assessing right into the physical space of the studio. As you enter the studio doorway, you walk up an accessible ramp that directs you around sharp corners, left and right, like a marble slowly making its way through a maze. We built this pathway to model this important need to slow down and consider the choices that lead to mature decisions.

Emerging leaders not only need self-assessment and self-correction; they also need external assessment and external correction. No matter how much we cultivate our self-knowledge and awareness, if we are to develop as leaders we need insight, reflections and feedback from others. Whether we are talking about shaping character, building competence or sustaining cadence, one thing holds true: we cannot read our own story accurately. Learning how to embrace feedback from others, early on, is a critical piece of leadership development for emerging leaders. Feedback is a recurring theme in this book because I believe it is at the heart of leadership development. The "Supporting Young People as They Succeed and Fail" chapter in section 4 includes a number of specific strategies on feedback to create learning and self-knowledge for young people.

How do we know when emerging leaders are really developing this competence of self-knowledge? One of the most powerful demonstrations is when they have the wisdom to say "I need help." This gift of asking grows from genuine self-knowledge. In our work on competency and leadership development, this is the early destination we want to get to with emerging leaders. We want them to be able to see, through both self and external assessment and correction, that they may have great vision or great communication or great organization—but their competency needs to grow with wisdom and experience. We want them not to fear to ask for help, for insight, for feedback. With that disposition, we can then accompany them through a well-staged path of competence development. Making mature choices is an overflow of a profound knowledge of self. This self-knowledge is built not only through personal reflection but also through candid and consistent feedback.

COLLABORATION—TO MOBILIZE COLLECTIVE STRENGTHS

An emerging leader in my circle went to a conference headlined by a dynamic young leader. When I asked about the conference experience, he told me, "John, it was really weird. He was the MC. He was the music leader. He was the speaker. And I thought to myself, did he really have to be up on the stage the whole time?"

In my experience, this pattern is not unusual. Time and time again, young people come to me and say, "I'll just do it, because I don't have time to teach someone else." Emerging leaders need exposure to a wide variety of experiences, but their tendency is to want to do everything themselves. They often tend to overestimate their own gifting and strengths. Further, they are inclined to say that it's easier just to do it themselves. There's an old story about building a house on rock or sand. It may be faster and quicker to build it on the sand, but when the storm comes, it will disappear. Quick and fast is the enemy of competence building.

> *"Sometimes, like before this program, when I would be in leadership situations, I would try to lead every aspect of things. And if someone was leading games, I would have to be there running games. Then if someone was running a small group, I would have to be leading that too. But it's so much easier, and so much more beneficial, and so much more effective for leaders to step back and divide into groups, so that are all assigned to a specific task. That way, they can put all of their heart into that one task, and it can be done so much more effectively and to a better standard."*—**CHEN**

Authentic leaders—who know both their strengths and weaknesses—will quickly know whether they are the right person to take on a task or manage a situation. Then, drawing from their deep self-knowledge about their own gaps, they will be able to identify the needed strengths and collaborate with others.

"Personally, I think one of the biggest leadership competencies I've developed is just learning more about myself. I'm normally a very independent person, so just by being able to look at myself now and say, 'Well, I can't do everything on my own,' and building teams around that, I can help myself."—**BEN**

Many young people confuse leadership with being up front. Or they believe leadership means "I'm the only one who can do it." But no one wants to work with a leader who takes away other people's opportunities or strengths or gifts. Instead of controlling the stage, the best leaders know who they are and who they're not. Then, they are liberated to collaborate with others and build others up. In fact, when the task is done, their friendships with others on their team are richer.

"I think to be a good leader, you have to also accept everyone's ideas. So it's not like you're the big boss. You have to listen to what others have to say if you're working in a team. But then again, you can't be a pushover. You have to set the standard and let your team know what you want done. So then that way, they will accomplish it, according to what standards you've set."—**CATHERINE**

Early on, young leaders need to learn to lead from their own strengths. However, a foundational element of competence is not only knowing how to offer help *to* others but also knowing when to ask for help *from* others. Young leaders need to practice this right from the start, even in small ways. Ironically, your greatest weakness is often your strength pushed without bounds. The most effective leaders let others step up into challenging assignments so they can mobilize collective strengths through collaboration.

MANAGING COMPLEXITY WITH A LEARNING DISPOSITION

The basic competence for personal leadership is self-knowledge. Layered on that, the basic competence for team leadership is collaboration. Emerging leaders often don't get into the world of organizational leadership until they are in their late twenties or thirties. However, in order to equip them for that time, we need to build within them, from the start, a learning disposition.

Research confirms that young people want to be mentored. Yet, when they get into a mentoring situation, they often resist the insights and urgings of the mentor. Personal humility—the ability to say "You have experience that I can learn from" or "I have as many questions as answers"—opens up young people to feedback, wisdom and growth. Personal humility is the fertile earth in which a learning disposition grows.

Personal humility is incredibly important at the organizational level. If you base your leadership on being the smartest person in the room and shutting off criticism, you will grip the organization too tightly and fail it in the end. But if you say "I don't have the answers" and instead offer questions—then you will get the input of others and build a collaborative culture.

Many leaders arrive at organizational leadership under horrendous pressure to do the right thing and have all the right answers. Yet change and complexity are a part of every enterprise. At the level of self-leadership, we have a fair degree of control on our response to change. At the team level, control and influence start to ebb. But at the organizational level, when change comes from all sides, the leader has little control. Good leaders will nurture a culture of learning, knowing how to ask "Have we got this right? Is this getting us the results we want?" And they will have the personal humility to admit "This isn't working for us; let's go back and look at this again." Particularly at the level of organizational leadership, dealing with complexity shows up as an ability to manage complexity, navigating systems, culture and diversity.

CULTIVATING THE BASICS
SO OTHER COMPETENCIES CAN GROW

When I assumed responsibility for the organizational life of Muskoka Woods, I had a three-year university degree, no business background and limited exposure to marketing and financial management. Early in my career in the camping industry, I met with the CEO of a large North American camping organization.

He reminded me that to be the CEO of a camp means to be CEO of a child-care service, a school, a health-care service, a restaurant, a hotel, a sports centre, an artists' studio, a property maintenance shop…and on it went. I quickly realized I did not have the competence on my own to manage all of these elements. Over and over, striving to anchor myself in a learning disposition, I go back again to my three basic questions: What competence is needed? Who has it? And how do we bring it to bear in this situation?

There are a multitude of lists of needed competencies that could be applied to the young emerging leader. But the three basics—self-awareness for mature decision making, collaboration for mobilizing collective strengths and a learning disposition for managing complexity—are the foundation from which other more specific competencies spring. These are the competencies needed early in the life of emerging leaders to cultivate and grow. This is how they can narrow the angle and respond to a multitude of different leadership challenges. If we build those basics well in their late teens and early twenties, we will set them up for effective leadership in their thirties, forties and beyond.

Chapter 4

CADENCE

Sustaining Leadership by Keeping in Step with Yourself, Others and God

UNDERSTANDING CADENCE AND SINGING FROM A BIGGER SONG SHEET

We all get compliments in our life. The greatest compliment I have ever received is when a friend who had just completed a consulting assignment for us said to me, "You kind of remind me of Bono."

Best known as the lead vocalist and songwriter for the Irish rock band U2, Bono is also well-known the world over as an activist and a humanitarian.

When I was a teenager living in Northern Ireland, I turned on the television and caught a glimpse of a U2 concert at Queen's University in Belfast. I made my way to the local record store and bought their first album on Chrono 1+1 cassette tape. At that point, they were so unknown that the cassette had U2 on one side, and the other side was blank.

Their music resonated deeply with me. At that time, in our polarized Northern Irish environment, we were never quite sure where U2 stood. Were they Nationalists? Were they Republicans? Did they stand on

KEY MESSAGES

- Cadence is keeping in step with yourself, others and God.

- The dispositions of openness, awareness and responsiveness help get us in cadence.

- Being in cadence sustains our leadership over the long term.

53

the Catholic side or the Protestant side? The night the *Joshua Tree* album was released, my police colleagues and I drove down in our police van to see the lineup outside the record store. It was huge, snaking around blocks and corners. I remember thinking to myself, *Wow, hundreds of Catholic and Protestant young people are standing together.* Even from the beginning, U2's music was trying to shape us all to a new way of thinking—that you didn't have to pick sides. You could be a bridge and live in the in-between. This band was pulling us together.

Bono has continued to intrigue and fascinate me over the years. I have followed his career and loved his music for decades. Who else can stand in front of 70,000 people at the Roger's Centre in Toronto and burst into "Amazing Grace" and have the whole crowd join in? Although Bono's life and my life are vastly different, I still relate to him. We both grew up Irish in the same time period. With a Protestant mother and a Catholic father, Bono certainly knows what it is like to grow up in the in-between. Different groups still try to claim him—Christians, humanitarians, politicians—but he refuses to be captive to a single label.

Bono doesn't know it, but my definition of leadership is profoundly informed by his life and influence on me. When he yells out at the end of "Sunday Bloody Sunday," "No more! No more!" or when he closes off his concerts with the haunting repeating line of "40," "How long will we sing this song...?" I am brought again to the way I describe leaders—*leaders look at their world and say "it doesn't have to be this way" and do something about it.*

U2 puts on a fantastic concert—high energy, loud, with an epic scale—and Bono will often talk before or in the middle of a song. When U2 was doing the Elevation Tour, before launching into "Where the Streets Have No Name," he would shout in the microphone some version of these words: "What can I give back to God for the blessings he's poured out on me? I'll lift high the cup of salvation—a toast to God! I'll pray in the name of God; I'll complete what I promised God I'd do, and I'll do it together with his people."

Bono is quoting not his own song but an ancient psalm. The words are taken from Psalm 116, a Jewish poem found in the Bible. When Bono yells out words of praise and promise from the Bible in the middle of a rock show, you realize that there is something bigger at stake for him. Not only is he singing his own song, he's also singing off a different song sheet. He's in step with something bigger than himself.

As a leader, I need something bigger than myself, something that helps me not to lose hope, something to sustain me, something that grounds me in a story bigger than my own. I need "to sing a new song," like Bono sings about in "40," which is a riff from Psalm 40. I need to be in rhythm with something greater than my own heartbeat. I call that experience of being in rhythm "cadence."

Most leadership models talk about character and competence, but *cadence* is an unusual word, even for me initially. The word first came to me on my sabbatical. In a calm and quiet space, in an unexpected whisper, I realized that I needed cadence.

What the word meant snapped into clarity for me when my best friend Paul's son had his 11th birthday party. In true Canadian style, the birthday party celebration began with some road hockey in the driveway. Before long, a shots competition had begun with one of the boys in net. When Paul walked out of the house to cheer on progress, he could immediately see that something was wrong: his son wasn't in the driveway. Instead, he was slumped against a tree on the opposite side of the yard, his back to the action. Paul walked past the group of boys enjoying the game to ask his son, "What's going on?" His son responded with a report of how the game wasn't fair, one of the boys had cheated, no one was playing right and so on. Paul said, "Look, this is your birthday. This is a celebration of you. Everyone else is having fun, but you're slumped against a tree closed to it all. You have got to get on the same page as what is going on here."

His son looked up at him, tears in his eyes, and said, "Dad, help me get on the same page."

Getting on the same page—that's cadence.

The word *cadence* comes from the Latin *cadenza,* a musical term that literally means falling. Cadence is falling in step or keeping in step with the rhythm, pace and flow around you.

Cadence is a beautiful concept for thinking about leadership development with emerging leaders. We need to keep in step with ourselves—knowing who we really are (and who we are not), how we are wired and how that drives the way we view the world. We need to keep in step with others—seeing young people for who they are, knowing their strengths and understanding the world they live in. And we also need to keep in step with God—alive to our own spirit and the Spirit around us.

Cadence is profoundly interconnected with both character and competence. I lead with great character and competency only when I am in cadence with myself, others and God. And when I am out of cadence, my leadership is in great danger of collapse.

55

Early in my professional life, I learned some hard personal lessons about being out of cadence. By the time I hit my mid-twenties, I was being given many opportunities to speak publically, at meetings, conferences and events. The problem was, despite the large number of opportunities, I somehow thought that every time someone invited me to speak, I should accept. So when a large youth organization asked me to be the main speaker at their conference in Florida, of course I said yes. It was the first time I was being paid to travel and speak, and I felt both excited and anxious. I knew that the way the conference participants judged the success of their week was going to be directly connected to how well I spoke each day.

I left the conference satisfied, but with a sore throat. Within weeks of returning home, I was on the road again, and my speaking schedule continued to pick up pace. My sore throat didn't get better but got worse, until I had sores on my throat that were so painful it was difficult to swallow. I went to an ear, nose and throat specialist, who wanted to do a biopsy. Through the course of our appointment, he asked me what was going on in my life. I told him I was recently married, my life was very busy, I had a constant stream of speaking engagements and so on. He said, "It sounds like you are under considerable stress."

It was the first time I had really heard that word: *stress*. When I asked my own doctor about the specialist's diagnosis he told me, "If you get in your car and push your accelerator flat to the floor and don't engage the gears, the engine will eventually blow up. But, if you engage the gears, the engine will last. Stress happens when you put the pedal to the metal for too long but don't engage the proper gear."

A friend echoed his words as we sat in a restaurant one afternoon after my appointment. He told me that he had met a lot of young leaders like me in their twenties who by the time they got to their thirties had burned out. He said, "You're saying yes to every invitation, you're on the road too much of the time and you have no criteria about what is the right event, the right subject or the right people."

My life was out of cadence. I was out of step with the right kind of rhythm for my unique calling and my distinctive competencies. As a result, it was starting to show up in my body. To sustain my development as a leader, I had to get back in step with myself, with others and with God.

How do we find cadence? Let me suggest three dispositions that, whether you are leading at the personal, team or enterprise level, will keep you in cadence with the rhythm and flow of what is happening in and around you. These dispositions are openness, awareness and responsiveness.

WALKING THE LEARNER PATH WITH A DISPOSITION OF OPENNESS

The first week of summer camp at Muskoka Woods is surging with energy and expectation. Staff are fresh; ideas are new; hopes are high. There's great openness to learning and new ideas. But then week two comes, and week three and week four. Mistakes, disappointment and fear enter in. Things may not have gone as expected. Instead of being open to learning from feedback, staff may be defensive. They begin to assume constraint, believing there's nothing they can do to bring about the change they want. Most significantly, their hope about what is possible has eroded. In short, in a matter of weeks, emerging leaders have moved from an open state to a closed one. What happened?

Author and management expert Ken Blanchard has developed a vocabulary for this progression. Blanchard's situational leadership theory is premised on the idea that leadership styles need to be tailored to particular situations, and he names four basic development levels: enthusiastic beginner, disillusioned learner, capable but cautious performer and self-reliant achiever/peak performer. Each development stage requires a different kind of leadership support. In week one of camp, staff are in the enthusiastic beginner stage, and they need "directing"—their skills and enthusiasm need to be acknowledged, and they need to be given some great plans and direction for how they will apply them. But as the days and weeks wear on, staff can enter the disillusioned learner stage. At that point, they need "coaching." Loss of hope and a closed state will not allow a leader to bring change. A big part of working with emerging leaders is to consistently invite them back to an open state. When coaches provide perspective, get them to reflect and ask questions, and cast a vision for new possibilities, we can then cultivate openness.

Being in cadence begins with a disposition of openness—openness to our own story and how that impacts every fibre of our being and doing, openness to the feedback of others to help us read our own story more accurately, and openness to God, whose story is far bigger than ourselves. The challenge is that many of us go through lives in a closed state—psychologically closed, physically closed, spiritually closed. We're not even on the same page as ourselves, much less the young people we are trying to inspire! Too often we are closed to others, not recognizing what our team can offer or where our enterprise is heading and how we fit with it all. Moreover, we are closed to God. We are not awake to the ways that God is working in our lives and in our world.

How do leaders maintain a disposition of openness? I take wisdom from my good friend Dr. Marilee Adams, who wrote *Change Your Questions: Change Your Life* in 2004. One of her basic concepts is that moment by moment, including every decision point and every challenge, we choose if we want to walk along a learner path or a judger path.

The paths are marked by questions. The learner path asks questions like "What works? What's possible? What are the facts, and what can I learn?" By contrast, the judger path asks questions like "Whose fault is it? How can I prove I'm right? What's wrong here?" Learner questions open doors; judger questions slam them shut. At the end of the judger path is the judger pit. Depending on the path we choose, we create different worlds to live in. The learner method opens us up to possibilities. The judger method erects stop signs.

Unfortunately, many of us are more hardwired to choose the judger than the learner path. Instead of being learners, we are too often judgers, inflating others' faults while emphasizing our own virtues. But we don't need to live that way.

One of the gifts God gives us is the capacity to discern our dominant style and alter our behaviour. Instead of continuing to travel down the judger lane, we can switch lanes. We can honestly ask "Am I a judger? Do I like how I feel? Do I like how I am affecting others? How else can I think about this? Am I pleased with the way I am leading?"

Changing our behaviour is difficult. But one of our "self-leadership" challenges is to monitor our methods. Changing lanes from being a judger to becoming a learner will take time and intentional effort, but the consequences will be dramatic.

> *"The biggest thing I learned is, as a leader and as a person, every morning you wake up, every task you do, you need to ask, what's possible? Because if you don't understand what's possible, what you're possible of or what your team's possible of, then you're never going to reach your highest goals. So, first, asking what's possible, and second, asking what you're willing to put in."*—**SOPHIA**

Living and leading with the openness of a learner is critical for cadence. Without openness, we risk staying in Blanchard's stage of disillusioned learner and never growing into the two development stages that are further along his path, capable but cautious performer and self-reliant achiever/peak performer. We need the kind of self-learning and openness that comes from walking the learner path, because leadership is not about having the answers. Rather, it is about being open to the idea that you may not know what is going on, you are unaware of what is best and you may be wrong. One of the most important results of living with a disposition of openness is maintaining your hope and passion for the idea that change is possible and you can do something about it.

Are you open?

STAYING AWAKE TO FRAMEWORKS WITH A DISPOSITION OF AWARENESS

Leaders find cadence when they live with a disposition of openness, to self, others and God. But maintaining an open state is also closely related to living with a disposition of attentiveness, particularly to our frameworks for seeing the world.

We often think that the job of a leader is to frame—a problem, a decision, an action. However, more often the job of the leader is not to put the frame up but to deconstruct it. Our tendency is to bring our story, our framework, our way of seeing to any given situation—and then to assume that others share the same view, and if not, they should! Instead, living with a posture of attentiveness means we are awake to our own framework and open to other people's ways of seeing, other people's gifts and other people's stories. Only by being both open and attentive will a leader be able to bring together all of people's best strengths and live in cadence.

Leadership is about change, but so often there is something underneath that counters our ability to make change. Being able to define the framework through which we are seeing reality and to discern what lies underneath is the posture of being attentive. The attentive leader asks "What is going on here? What do I really want? What do others want? What hidden framework is driving our decision making? What's next?" To live with a disposition of attentiveness means to be able to take down assumptions and make sure that we are not defining things by our limited frameworks.

> *"As a leader, take in and listen to what people say. And upon that make a final decision. Before my involvement in the CEO program, one of my weakest traits was decision making. And I definitely think that I've improved there."*—**ERIC**

When working with emerging leaders to help them develop a disposition of attentiveness, I sometimes use a mentoring reflective pathway that I developed with Jack McQueeney, my colleague in the camping industry. The pathway helps the leaders reflect on events and their impact—particularly, the gap between what happened and what the young person expected to happen. The gap is always around the idea of expectations and perceptions. The frameworks we create to interpret experience are often full of distortions, deletions, exaggerations and generalizations. What we are trying to do is get an emerging leader to move through reflection like this: *I believed this was happening; I acted; this was the result I got; it didn't work out the way I wanted. What were my assumptions? What was my inner critic saying? What did others believe was really going on? What signs did I see or not see? What beliefs were informing my actions?* When we are attentive, we can reflect on these kinds of questions and turn them into new learning that we can then apply to new events.

To have leadership cadence, we need more than our own narrative. We need feedback and input. Otherwise, our tendency is to create a narrative driven by our change agenda. When we rely solely on our self-perceptions we close the door to input from others. When we surrender ourselves to feedback from others around us, we gain a "wider lens" that can lead to alternative responses.

We also need to be attentive to the frameworks we are using to define our reality and be prepared to take them down. Openness reaffirms a belief that life doesn't have to be this way and we can do something about it. But we need attentiveness to keep us awake to questions like "Am I sure that my own narrow frame isn't defining this situation? What do I need to do for my team and my organization in this moment? From a position of knowing my authentic self and what others can bring, what role do I now play?"

Are you attentive?

MOVING TO ACTION WITH A DISPOSITION OF RESPONSIVENESS

Now open, now aware, leaders must next be responsive. What use is a posture of responsiveness if we are not also ready to move? "Keeping in step" with the rhythm and flow of life and leadership implies action. Responsiveness is where openness and attentiveness meet practical reality. Will you act on what you now know to be true? Action takes hope and courage—and that ability to embolden courage to respond is one of the marks of a leader.

I was sailing with three of my friends on Lake Rosseau, and we got into the doldrums—there was no wind. We sat there for several minutes. When I looked across the lake, I saw that the water had begun to change shape about 400 yards away, and I realized we were going to get wind. I was open and attentive enough to see that a new reality was about to blow down on us. So I turned the boat, and as soon as I felt the wind on the back of my head, I braced. The boat went up on its edge, and everyone else grabbed something to steady themselves. Then we began to fly across the water.

I have enough experience sailing that I can anticipate the moment to respond to take advantage of a coming wind and get out of the doldrums. But many emerging leaders who are still learning to live in cadence need an encouraging push to respond, especially when responding may mean taking a difficult stand. When working with emerging leaders, we need to nurture in them the courage to respond to problems early, before they are in too much pain and it becomes too late, and before an acute problem becomes chronic. When huge ships are headed on journeys between continents, even a miscalculation of one or two degrees will have a radical impact on where they will arrive. So also, we need to encourage emerging leaders to respond early, before the long-term effects are very difficult to correct. To act and be responsive, emerging leaders need vision and hope about what is possible. That vision, alongside support and encouragement, is what spurs them to say "I need to act now." Responsiveness then builds their muscles for resilience.

The reality is that leaders often step into situations where they do not have the resources they need. At that point, open to their own unfinished nature, attentive to the gifts and strengths of those around them, alive to a vision of what is possible and supported with encouragement, leaders need to respond with a step of faith. Turn the boat, put out the sail and hold on.

Are you responsive?

DESIGNED TO BE IN CADENCE

We are designed to be in cadence—in step with ourselves, with others and with God. Without cadence, our bodies can break down, our relationships can be disregarded or damaged and our inner lives can be cracked and dry. Our leadership needs to be sustained by something beyond our own limited skills, energies and frameworks. We need to be in step with something deeper than ourselves.

One of the great discoveries of my Christian tradition is that we can only live well and lead well when we know that we are loved more than we can imagine. I find great solace in the words of Psalm 139, where the poet writes of how we are deeply known and treasured—"You created my inmost being; you knit me together in my mother's womb. I praise you because I am fearfully and wonderfully made." We also hear this message of unimaginable love echoed by some of the great spiritual writers. Henri Nouwen, for example, was an internationally renowned author, professor and priest. At the encouragement of his friends, he published his "secret journal" in which he wrote about the most anguished and difficult period of his life, when he had lost his hope and energy to live and work. He called this book *The Inner Voice of Love*. It was that inner voice that sustained him through the darkest of times.

Emerging leaders need to understand that they are deeply loved and championed for who they are. You cannot relate to young people unless you are open, attentive and responsive to yourself and unless you are open, attentive and responsive to them. If you do not see and appreciate where they are at, you will never be able to nurture the trust that is required to coach or mentor a young person in his or her leadership development. As long as you insist to young people that they need to be at a certain place before you will come alongside them, you will meet resistance. Instead, emerging leaders need to know that they are loved, known and not alone. They need to tune in to and be reminded of the inner voice of love.

An old story speaks of an eagle that is born and raised among chickens. He spends his days clucking and pecking at scattered seed. One day, he looks up and sees another eagle, flying high over the treetops and swooping low over the farm. He realizes that he is born to soar, but he's spending his days wandering in the dirt of the barnyard. Emerging leaders are designed to soar. They are designed to be in step with the rhythm and flow of themselves, others and God. They are designed to be in cadence.

Section III

SPANNING THE DISTANCE

Maximizing Influence with Emerging Leaders

Chapter 5

WALKING WITH YOUNG PEOPLE IN THE IN-BETWEEN

The Role of Mentors, Coaches and Sages

KEY MESSAGES

- The roles of mentor, coach and sage have distinct paradigms and best practices, as well as their own virtues and vulnerabilities.

- When leadership developers work at their best, they are often dancing and weaving between the three roles.

- Mentors, coaches and sages show up well for emerging leaders when they model how to define reality, live as a learner and be authentic.

VIRTUES AND VULNERABILITIES OF MENTORS, COACHES AND SAGES

During my first winter in Canada, a friend said to me, "Let's walk across the lake to the other side." He began striding confidently out across the ice, but I stood, frozen to the shoreline. He turned around and said, "What are you doing? Come on!" Only when I saw a vehicle driving across the lake did I gingerly put out my foot and begin to follow.

The first-time journey of a Northern Irishman across a frozen Canadian lake is a good analogy for understanding the roles of mentor, coach and sage. How do we get emerging leaders to move, to take a step into new and uncertain territory? How do we develop in them those footings of cadence, character and competence?

The mentor says, "Walk with me. Follow me; I've done this before. I have experience; this is the way that you plant your feet on an icy surface." And as the mentor walks across the frozen lake, I venture out from shore and watch and learn from his or her expertise.

The coach says, "I will walk with you." And as the journey continues, the coach

65

invites me to talk about whatever I want to in that moment. Rather than playing the role of the ice-walking expert, the coach realizes that I am the expert in my own story, because I am the only one who has ever experienced it. As we walk together across the lake, I may become overwhelmed by cold and fear and whatever else is going on in my life. The coach taps into where he or she has experienced fear before and helps me find my courage and reserves and resources to continue the journey.

The sage says "Let's walk with wisdom." This wisdom has many sources that are around us but also beyond us. Wisdom can be found in sacred writings, in the lives of worthy models and in biographies of people who have lived well. The ultimate wisdom comes from God as we walk our faith alongside people around us and strive to be effective in our daily responsibilities. The sage is the one who helps us discern and discover where God is on this journey across the ice.

Mentor, coach, sage—each makes it across the lake with the young person, and each can help develop the footings of character, competence and cadence. But each walks with a different gait, and each has virtues and vulnerabilities.

MENTORS

The virtue of mentors is their experience. Mentors have been there before. They have lived the ins and outs of various problems, and they have learned what helps people move ahead and what gets people stuck. They have expertise and insight and can act as a trusted guide.

The vulnerability of the mentor is to presume expertise and to exert too much force in another person's life. There's lots of research out there that says young people want to be mentored. Indeed, mentorship can be a powerful role. Sometimes, too powerful. There are certain people in my life whom I never go to for advice on certain subjects, because their influence on me is so powerful that I would be captive to their opinion. They have too much latent weight, and thus I shut out my own voice from the conversation. Instead of empowering me in that moment, they actually disempower. When an expert is in the room, people easily wave the white flag and surrender to the expert's opinion. As mentors, we need to be highly aware of our own power.

People whose role is to develop young leaders often overuse the mentor role. For every problem or challenge a young person is experiencing, we become an expert in that thing. The problem is that when we overuse the expert mentor role, young people shut down. The tendency of the mentor is to solve people's problems too quickly and presume that their experience and expertise are the right ones for the young person. One of the most important things we can give to a young emerging leader is often not to give direction and answer the questions but instead to ask them. "What ideas do you have? Which options seem to be the best? What might get in your way?"

COACHES

The virtue of coaches is their accompaniment. Coaches do three simple things: they listen, they ask and they speak. Melinda Sinclair is a master certified coach who has worked with Muskoka Woods over the past few years. She puts it this way: "Coaching is about the connection between a person who wants to change something (the coachee) and someone who is willing to facilitate this change process (the coach). The connection happens in conversation." The quality of the connection is what creates the space for change and growth.

As a method of leadership development, coaching is still in an adolescence stage. Yet, the more we lean on a coaching disposition, the greater the opportunity for learning for a young person. Coaching is predominantly about how to use questions rather than how to give answers. It's both a methodology and a disposition that involves staying with a young person as they walk through an experience and moving with them as they solve their issues themselves. Coaches don't jump ahead but walk alongside. Coaching a young emerging leader involves cultivating a genuine conversation that allows you to get further into their story.

	VIRTUE	VULNERABILITY
MENTOR	Experience	Presume Expertise
COACH	Accompaniment[3]	Problem Solving
SAGE	Wisdom	Project Their Own Story

---

3 "Accompaniment" was first used by Paul Johansen.

The vulnerability of the coach is to problem solve. Rather than to listen, ask and speak, the coach can sometimes speak, ask and listen. I've seen this dynamic many times at Muskoka Woods, where we use a "one-on-one" coaching model. Each week, every staff person meets one-on-one for 30 to 60 minutes with someone else on staff who serves as a coach. The person in the coaching role has more experience and is more mature than the person they meet with. The model is used from the president right down to the youngest staff person. The goal is for every person to have someone they can go to who knows them and supports them.

When we first started, we found that staff coaches often came to the one-on-one meeting with the disposition of "Here's what I want to teach you today." In other words, the coaches were speaking first, instead of listening first. They were defaulting into a more expert mentor role, rather than a coaching role. By presuming they already knew what to teach, they were unintentionally robbing the young leaders of their reflective self. The consequence of prejudging what people needed to learn was that we often missed the pieces that people needed to move forward in their own leadership development. Instead of accompanying them in their process of problem solving, we were hijacking their story with the solution. But if a coach communicates learning that is not discovered or owned by the person being coached through his or her own process of reflection, that learning is far less likely to bring about change.

So we taught and reinforced a better coaching disposition, beginning with listening. It's not "Here's what I am going to teach you" but instead "What do you want to focus on today? What more can you tell me about this? How is this affecting you? What role would you like to play to impact this situation?"

SAGES

The virtue of the sage is to access wisdom and insight. Sages find the deeper meaning in ordinary things. They often make their contribution in the moment. The sage is the one who is able to recognize that there are three people in the room, not two; there is something or someone bigger than you and me. Still, sages are human. They can be vulnerable to transferring their own experiences into the circumstances of the younger leaders they are seeking to serve.

There is a long tradition of the role of the sage in many religious frameworks, including Christianity and Judaism. Sages take on a function of spiritual direction, walking with people in their ordinary experience and helping reveal the extraordinary presence of God in that person's life. Sages crave a lively and intimate relationship with God and help deepen and grow that relationship for others. They help nurture the inner life with God, and in so doing they are able to reveal insight that is beyond human understanding.

Because of their ability to nurture the inner life, many sages have lived deeply and may have incredible learning to contribute to young people about how to nurture character, competence and cadence. But any insight from a sage needs to flow from a deep appreciation of where the young person is in their unique journey. Sages have to be careful that they do not project their story onto someone else. If the sage's insights don't resonate with a young person's personal story, the young person will shut down or run.

BLENDING ROLES AND MODELING LEADERSHIP

When I first learned to be a police diver at 19, an old salty dog took me under his wing. He was one of the most experienced search and rescue divers in the country, and I was one of the youngest. In the downtime between dives, he would often sit on the side of the boat and make knots. When you watched him tie them with such grace and fluidity, you wanted to do the same. He had an incredible ability to tie the right knot at the right time.

In ancient days, coastal communities used ropes for three things. The first was to open and close sails. The second was to plumb the depths. And the third was to secure the anchor. The ability to discern what a young person needs in this moment is a finely tuned skill that requires incredible appreciation for the environment, as well as a deep understanding of the young person. The art is to be able to throw the right rope at the right time. Do they have the character that is required to pull in the sails and steer in the right direction? Do they have the competence they need to swim at this depth, or are they in over their head? Are they anchored in a healthy cadence? In this moment, to get where they need to go, what role moves them ahead: the coach, the mentor or the sage?

A lot of young people come into my life and say, "I want you to mentor me." Or "I want you to coach me." Or "I want you to give me spiritual direction." The reality is, I often end up doing all three. That's being a blended developer—and it's the best way to meet young people where they are at and help them get where they need to go.

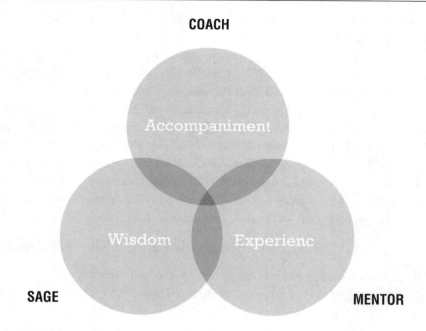

COACH

Accompaniment

Wisdom   Experienc

SAGE   **MENTOR**

When you map coach, mentor and sage in a Venn diagram, at the centre is what looks like a Celtic knot, where all three overlap. A biblical proverb says, "A chord of three strands is not quickly broken" (Ecclesiastes 4:12), and the same is true here. At our best, we blend and weave between these three roles, depending on the situation, the person and the need.

Although each role has its distinct paradigm and distinct best practices, the best of all worlds is when you blend them together and move and dance naturally between them. Jesus is a clear example. Remember, most of the disciples were young people. Jesus was at times a mentor—teaching the disciples to pray, for example. He was at times a coach—asking them questions that helped them figure out what was going on in their own lives. And he was often and always a sage.

When you are working at your best, you will be a blended developer—knowing when to be a mentor, adding experience; knowing when to be a coach, walking alongside; and knowing when to be a sage, creating space for people to see where God is in that moment. If we can learn to weave between all three roles well, then we will able to show up in a much more powerful way to elevate and enhance leadership development for young people.

Eddie Officer was one of the early blended developers in my life. Eddie was a youth leader who would take me and my friends into the mountains of Northern Ireland on camping trips. We would exit the van at a place called Bloody Bridge. We were young guys with energy and all of the right gear—gators and Gortex jackets. He was slow and methodical, with an old canvas backpack and weatherworn leather boots. When we arrived at the base of a big wooded hill, he told us, "You can take the path on the left or the right."

The left pathway looked wider and faster, so that was our choice. To our surprise, he chose the narrower right-hand path and told us he'd see us at the top. Half an hour later, we were reunited at the crest of the hill, but he was in a considerably different state than we were. We had walked up an old quarry road made for big trucks, but he had followed the sheep path. Our path ended up being twice the distance, but his was through soft heather and was the shortest way up. From that moment on, I watched him closely and listened intently to his well-measured words. He became the model mountaineer for me, and I diligently learned from him and, literally, walked in his footsteps.

Whether I am acting in the role of mentor, coach or sage for a young emerging leader, I am ever and always modeling. In everything I do as a leadership developer with young people, I need to presume that they will walk in my footsteps and replicate them to the young people under them. No matter which rope I am throwing, no matter which role I am playing, the young leaders I am developing are likely to forge a path similar to the one I have shown them.

Regardless of the specific task at hand, mentors, coaches and sages show up well for emerging leaders when they model some distinctive behaviours and dispositions. These modeled behaviours match the things we are trying to cultivate with emerging leaders as we build the footings of character, competence and cadence. The same lens that we apply to emerging leaders, we need to also apply to those who are shepherding their development. I want to highlight three particular practices to model that have the deepest impact for emerging leaders: defining reality, living as a learner and being authentic.

DEFINING REALITY BY READING THE LANDSCAPE

Max De Pree, in *Leadership Is an Art*, writes, "The first responsibility of a leader is to define reality. The last is to say thank you. In between, the leader is a servant."

Defining reality has been a recurring theme in this book. In chapter 2, about shaping character, I wrote about the important strategy of cultivating

71

attunement in emerging leaders. Attunement is that quality of being keyed into the reality at hand and knowing how to show up with your whole character so that you are part of the solution, not the problem. In chapter 3, about building competence, I talked about the importance of having the personal humility to recognize that the reality at hand may be more complex that one can easily decipher. And in chapter 4, about cultivating cadence, I talked about the disposition of attentiveness and being able to examine and break down the frameworks that we, often unconsciously, use to define our own reality.

Defining reality is about seeing the landscape and where you are in it. When I first started being trained as a police diver, one of the most frightening experiences was to be underwater in the pitch-dark. When you get vertigo underwater, you are inclined to go up too fast or down too far. Either way can be disastrous. That's why early on in your diving training you learn a set of simple practices so you can find your way in the dark. When you have vertigo and you don't know where you are, you take your depth gauge and put it right against your mask. When you see the depth gauge go up, you know you are headed in the direction of the surface; when you see it go down, you know you are heading toward the sea floor. The important discipline to learn is that you cannot listen to what is going on in your head—there's chaos and complexity and confusion there. Instead, you have to ruthlessly focus on reading the gauge, and that alone. Only then can you reconnect with your other points of contact to get your bearings and plot what is required next. Without grounding yourself first with the gauge, you become paralyzed by fear or anxiety and a narrative in your head that is not true.

Defining reality may seem a strange first task of leadership development, but it is one of the most important roles of a mentor, coach or sage in the life of a young leader. Emerging leaders often feel like they have vertigo. Because of their lack of experience, they will often plow into things without asking "Should I? Could I? Would I? What if?" Then, quite suddenly, they are in unfamiliar waters, without enough appreciation for the environment, and without a map. They don't know where they are, much less where they should go. Then, their inner dialogue takes control. Some are worried about lack of acceptance and failure. Others are just busy and without focus. At that point, the most critical task is to reorient them and help them define reality.

One of the most effective ways to define reality with emerging leaders is through a good conversation. Melinda Sinclair's five-step coaching conversation flow framework is a helpful tool. The first step is to "connect now." That's clueing in to the state and mood of your young leader and building rapport. The everyday things you do with young people are the materials for development. There is never a moment lost in working with younger leaders; you only need to see the opportunity. Much of my leadership development with young people has been in the moment.

The second step is to "clarify why," to position the focus of the conversation and what the coachee wants to gain. All coaching really begins with the question "What do you want?"

The third is to "create new." Here, the coaching conversation generates awareness, ideas and possibilities through questions and brainstorming. This is where defining reality really hits full steam. Great coaching questions at this stage include "What can you tell me about this? How is this affecting you? What have you tried? What are some other possibilities?"

Next, "choose what"—choose an action, explore the obstacles and figure out the plan of response.

And finally, "commit and go"—confirm the commitment and figure out how to get the right supports in place. The ultimate goal is to help people converse with the narrative in their head and to self-coach themselves in that moment.

Leaders often run into barriers that stop us from moving forward to the next level or from making the positive change we want to see. When we define reality through conversation and reflection, we begin to discover what is getting in our way, what beliefs and frameworks are informing our perceptions and what prompts and motivates us. When a young emerging leader is stuck or in vertigo, the role of the mentor, coach and sage is to help define reality for the young emerging leader so they can move ahead to the next step.

LIVING AS A LEARNER

When I teach leadership courses, the one consistent piece of feedback I get from my students is this: Thank you for telling me that I don't have all the answers; you've allowed me to see that unearthing the question and staying as a learner is more important.

The theme of living as a learner has already been visited several times in this book. In the character chapter, I wrote about the importance of learning and self-discovery. In the competence chapter, I named a learning disposition to manage complexity as one of the three basic competencies to cultivate. And in the cadence chapter, I wrote about the disposition of openness and walking on the learner path rather than the judger path. Leaders are not superhuman. They do not have perfect character, they cannot master every competency, they are sometimes out of cadence, and they cannot predict the future—especially in a world of chaos and complexity. And yet the image of a leader as strong, visionary and successful is so pervasive that many leaders succumb to the pressure of having to house within them all of the resources needed to bring positive change to every situation.

As mentors, coaches and sages for emerging leaders, we need to model a different image of a leader—the leader who lives as a learner. A learner has exceptional self-awareness and is open to feedback and reflection from others. A learner recognizes their own shortcomings and can tap into the collective strengths of others. A learner asks meaningful questions, listens, reads and reflects. A learner has authentic personal humility and has no fear of saying "I don't know" or "I need help in this area."

When young people come to us looking for help, we need to resist the temptation to overreach and overclaim our own capacity. Instead, we need to operate with a learning disposition that is ready to say "I don't have the answers…but let's figure out together what you need in this moment to move ahead."

One of the things I do as a Christian minister is meet with young couples before they get married and help prepare them for that adventure. But I don't take all of it on. When it comes to money management, I suggest consulting a financial adviser. When it comes to managing stress and pressure, I suggest a person the couple could talk to. When it comes to starting a new job, I suggest a particular book. In fact, you might say that my area of expertise is knowing who and how to ask for help. My role is to direct others to the right person or resource they need to move ahead, rather than do it all myself.

In any given stage of a young person's life, he or she probably only needs one coach and one sage, but they may need several mentors. Live with a learning disposition, and you will be able to discern where you can make a contribution in this young person's life and where you need to get out of the way.

ACTING WITH AUTHENTICITY

Just as we call emerging leaders to authenticity when we develop their character, competence and cadence, so also we need to model authenticity for them as mentors, coaches and sages. Bill George is professor of management practice at Harvard Business School, where he leads the program on authentic leadership development. In his bestselling book *True North*, he talks about staying the course to your own true north—your most deeply held beliefs, values and principles—even in the face of the most serious pressures and seductions. Only when you do that, he argues, are you able to gain the trust of others, which will allow you to motivate them to high performance.

Authenticity is absolutely critical when working with emerging leaders because it's all about trust. When young people sense a whiff of pretense or hypocrisy, you lose all ability to influence in that moment. Being authentic means acting in a way that is consistent with your true self. For Bill George, and I agree, the key to authenticity is self-awareness and feedback—understanding the arc of your own story and its impact in your life and leadership. You have to understand how to show up in a given situation and how your state of being contributes to what is going on. You cannot develop this self-awareness on your own. You also need the feedback and reflection of others. When you are not honest and true to yourself and you do not open yourself to feedback from others, you will slowly create a life of cover-up. Without awareness and authenticity what may begin as a natural fear may end up in a destructive response.

Early in my leadership journey, a colleague sent me a great article by email. He wrote with enthusiasm, "John, do you know this guy? You have to read this article." In fact, I did not know the author's work, but I read the article and agreed that it was great. I quickly did some research on the Internet and discovered that the author had written three other articles that were also well worth reading. At the next staff training meeting, I shared the article and my other Internet discoveries. But here's where I went wrong. When speaking at the staff meeting, I disguised my lack of prior knowledge about the author. Rather than saying "I had never seen this; thanks for sharing," I created an illusion that I was already in the know. Out of my own sense of insecurity, wanting to impress my staff, I acted in an inauthentic way.

After the meeting, my conscience kicked in. I knew I had not demonstrated the character I need to as a leader. So I wrote an email in response to the person who had sent me the article and confessed my inauthenticity. I then read my response out loud at the next staff meeting.

Even mature leaders are often tempted to posture. To create the illusion that they know more than they do, that they are more on top of things than they are. But there is a personal cost to not being authentic. It's not just the loss of influence and trust with others, though that is sure to come. The falseness eats you up. When you are not real and you are not honest and true to yourself, you are already beginning the process of undermining your trust with others and the health of your organization. Being authentic is about knowing your own strengths, but also your own weaknesses, blind spots and vulnerabilities. Authenticity is closely linked to character, because the authentic person has no gap between who they are when they are a leader on show in the world and who they are when they are on their own.

I draw a distinction between transparency and authenticity. There are times when being overly transparent can be destructive. There are situations where I can reveal too much. When I choose to be vulnerable with the young people I am mentoring, coaching or giving spiritual direction to, I ask myself three questions: Is what I am sharing of service to the other person (or is it of service to me)? Am I sure that I am not projecting my own story or my own fear or anxiety on other people? Is this the right time to share this information? If I can answer yes to these questions, I have confidence that I am not posturing or pretending to be who I am not but rather being authentic.

LEADERSHIP DEVELOPMENT FOR IN-BETWEEN PEOPLE

Emerging leaders are in-between people. They are not children but may not yet be fully independent adults. Their beliefs are in flux. They are still in the throes of identity formation. They are transitioning from family to autonomy. They are still building the footings of cadence, character and competence in their lives. When emerging leaders get stuck or they drift unmoored, that's where coaches, mentors and sages can model for them how to define reality, live with a learning disposition and be authentic. The same things we are trying to cultivate in emerging leaders, we also need to practice ourselves.

When we work with young people, we usually have a very limited period of time. Most of the emerging leaders that come into my life are in my orbit for four years or less before they move on. With emerging leaders, we need to have a clear idea of what outcomes we want for them. By the end of four years, what contribution do we want to make in their lives? People who are developing emerging leaders need to be able to answer this question: What is the best way for me to show up in the relationship to bring about the end goal? My hope is always that the young people I help develop can say "I was brilliantly managed and I was brilliantly coached around my work, personal growth and spiritual growth. As a result, without question, I am a better leader, ready and inspired to shape my world."

Section IV

TRANSVERSING TOGETHER

Positioning Emerging Leaders
for Exceptional Development

Chapter 6

SEEING YOUNG PEOPLE FOR WHO THEY ARE AND WHO THEY CAN BECOME

SEEING EMERGING LEADERS FOR WHO THEY CAN BECOME

When I was a kid, each weekday morning I would set off on the long walk to school. One day, I was halfway there before I realized that my family dog was following behind me. I immediately turned around, ran the dog back home and started the trek again at double pace. Despite coming at a run, I arrived after the bell and was sent immediately to the vice principal's office. He looked at me accusingly in the eye and demanded I explain why I was late. After I told him what happened with the dog, he stared piercingly at me and said, "You're big enough and ugly enough to know better." Those words burned into me, and I remember them sharply still.

In my early school years, my math teacher wrote of me, "John is very slow to grasp new concepts." Then, when I was 13, my French teacher reinforced the same feeling of failure. On the first day of class, he gave every student a test. He would assign seats according to the marks. I was in the third to last chair. That was the day

KEY MESSAGES

- Many emerging leaders get missed.

- Seeing young people means noticing, calling forth, highlighting and developing the strengths and potential in each person.

- Mentors, coaches and sages need to understand the landscape in which emerging leaders live and how it shapes their leadership challenges.

- When young people get the message "I see you, I believe in you," they are unleashed to discover their best selves.

79

I got the humiliating message loud and clear that I wasn't smart enough to do well in school.

I was an intensely verbal kid who had a hard time staying focused. My art teacher told me I talked too much and made me write out 500 times "I must not talk verbal diarrhea." I was continually punished because I was always distracted and never able to sit still.

I was an avid member of my school's canoeing and mountain clubs. Almost every other week, I would go up to the mountains of Northern Ireland. I was told, "John, if you don't stop going up the mountains camping, you're going to blow it on your schoolwork."

This is how many of the adults in my life saw me: a kid who was slow, a kid who talked too much, a kid who spent too much time in the woods. Now, what do I do for a living? I get paid to talk. I get paid to think differently. I get paid to oversee a camp. It was all there, but no one saw it. My career path and my gifts were laid out for all to see. But most people missed it. They didn't see or affirm my true character, my strengths, my abilities—and they certainly didn't see who I could become.

Thankfully, some did.

Because even as a kid, if you gave me a creative challenge, I would flourish. In high school my teacher assigned a project to use our imaginations to make whatever we wanted. "Let your creativity go wild." My dad worked for a company that supplied televisions. I got him to drop off a generous number of large television boxes at school, and my friends and I built and painted a huge model of the international space station. It was so amazing that everyone wanted to explore and play in the creation.

The organist at our church was also my religious education teacher. Charlie McGuiness was a teacher I loved. Although many of the guys in my class aimed to create havoc, I had been brought up to respect my elders—and that included Mr. McGuiness. At the end of my school year, he said to my mother unexpectedly, "John will make a fine minister one day." He saw me and what I could become.

Despite myself and despite my own lack of vision of what I would become, some people did see me and my strengths and potential. I did land a job where my creativity is given full reign. I don't build models of the space station, but I do dream up and put into action creative programs and ideas for young people at Muskoka Woods. Not only that, I did become a Christian minister. I now spend much of my time talking to people about who God is in their lives. God was calling me all along and drawing me in. Yet most of the adults around me were so stuck in their premade judgments of who I was that all they saw was a distracted kid who talked too much. They missed what I was going to become.

My story is not unique. Many emerging leaders get missed. This is a subject of great frustration for me. After all, how old do you think many of the disciples were? How old was Mary? How old was Jesus when he started teaching in the temple? Teenagers. Not fully formed. Not finished. Not fully mature. But full of gifts and potential.

Seeing young people means that we notice, call forth, highlight, encourage and develop the strengths and potential in each person. We need to believe in young people and see their ability to contribute. This takes individualized attention and intention—to both ourselves by the way that our judgments and preconceptions can paralyze our vision and to young people. Seeing young people is the first step to unlocking their potential. The next step is creating a space for them to succeed, fail and, above all, learn.

The truth is, it can be difficult to see the good in young leaders because it is often overshadowed by their immaturity and bravado. But one of the great disciplines in raising up new young leaders is not to write them off too quickly. We need to drop our judgments, drop our preconceived frames and open our minds, eyes and hearts to see emerging leaders for all they are and all they can become. One of the most important things that "older" leaders do is identify and develop the young people who come up behind them. It has to happen intentionally, or it will not get done. We need both willingness and openness to truly see young people.

UNDERSTANDING THE LANDSCAPE OF TODAY'S EMERGING LEADERS

One of the first things that mature mentors, coaches and sages have to realize as they develop younger emerging leaders is that this generation is not like others that have come before. A couple thousand years ago, Heraclitus cautioned us, "No one ever steps in the same river twice." It seems that change was constant in Ancient Greece, too. Then, as now, leaders waded into the river—but they needed to do it with eyes open to see the context. Not only do we need to see young people, we need to see the landscape they live in.

Each year, groups of young people take hiking and canoeing trips into Algonquin Park. One leader has been taking these groups for more than a decade. Each year, he has led the same route—the same wooded paths, lakes, rivers and rapids. But although the route is the same, the trip has an entirely different flavour from what it used to have. Why? The trip leader has observed that the groups of young people are not as fit as they used to be. They don't have the same level of trust of their leaders. They are not well equipped to deal with interpersonal conflict. It's Heraclitus' principle of the river. The world of young people has changed; so have they, and so have we.

This generation of young people lives in a different world than the one their parents grew up in. Their world is marked by several profound sociological trends, including pluralism, relativism, globalization and consumerism. They also live in a world of tremendous technological innovation, where social media and technology are an intimate part of their existence. They have grown up digital. Their immersion in technology is early and expansive. Anyone who has spent any time around young people will observe that it is not unusual for their cellphones to call them to attention literally hundreds of times a day.

The world that today's young people have inherited has a huge impact on what they believe and how they behave. In 2011, my colleague and youth expert Chris Tompkins, alongside Don Posterski and me, analyzed research from a sample of 235 young people and published the book *Elastic Morality: Leading Young Adults in Our Age of Acceptance*. The research highlights that today's young people operate with elastic morality—a mindset for right and wrong that creates space for diversity, resists judgment, extends uncensored acceptance, exchanges certainty for mystery and stretches the boundaries of belief and behaviour.

In other words, the vast majority of today's' young adults believe that it is far more important to accept others than to agree with them. In their view, championing one choice as superior to another smacks of arrogance. For all their virtues and vulnerabilities, today's young adults ardently embrace acceptance as their primary value.

This generation of young people typically has an incredibly difficult time speaking the truth to one another. In the name of acceptance, they will tolerate all kinds of actions and behaviour because they do not have the courage to walk in and say to a peer "I need a few minutes with you to talk about something." Instead, they will put off confrontation for weeks and months. There's an old Hebrew proverb that says "Better is open rebuke than hidden love. Wounds from a friend can be trusted, but an enemy multiplies kisses" (Proverbs 27:5–6). Today's young people find it extremely difficult to operate by that principle. They would rather be a friend and be accepted than a leader and be rejected.

But here's the challenge for emerging leaders: it is very difficult to be in leadership and not have to say at some point or another that this is the right way to go, and that is the wrong one. In fact, leaders are often called on to make decisions and to lead their followers in chosen directions. Unless you learn early in your leadership development how to say no with great comfort, you will significantly struggle later in your leadership. The ethos that emerging leaders live in makes it tempting for them to be character chameleons, becoming whatever they need to become to be accepted and saying what people want to hear rather than what they need to hear.

> *"Before CEO, I was very kind of, well, not a pushover, but I didn't like getting people angry. So I wouldn't really push things, and some people would kind of walk over me. Being here, it's truly taught me to be able to say no and just be able to set boundaries, because I've never been able to do that before. Even with my friends. I think that's going to help me later on."*—CAROLINE

The landscape that emerging leaders live in creates particular contours and obstacles that shape their leadership challenges and growth. For example, in a world where the power of acceptance is dominant, do emerging leaders have the character to stand up and lead in directions that may not have everyone's agreement? In a world whose pace is increasingly accelerated, do young leaders have the competence to slow down and reflect on what is truly needed? In a world of quick fixes and search-engine solutions, where busyness is a badge of honour, do young leaders have the cadence to develop deeply and sustain growth? Mentors, coaches and sages need not only to see young people themselves but also to be intent on reading the contextual realities they live in. Only then can we shape their leadership development effectively.

KNOWING THE PERSONAL STORY OF EMERGING LEADERS

Not only do we need to observe, study and understand the contextual landscape that emerging leaders live in, we also need to know the personal story of the emerging leaders we are developing. Seeing young people for who they really are and who they can become is a prerequisite for building trust and doing leadership development. The impact is two-way. When mentors, coaches and sages truly see young people, they can map out a path for stretching and supporting them in leadership development. Not only that, but when young people are truly seen, they grow in confidence and trust in themselves. With greater confidence, they are more willing to step out and be stretched. When young people get the message "I see you; I believe in you," that is when they are unleashed to discover their best selves.

Emerging leaders tend to be insistently relational. The vast majority of getting to know someone's story happens in the context of listening and conversation in everyday moments. However, there are also some excellent formal tools for emerging leaders that help develop their own self-awareness, reveal strengths and areas for growth and bring their personal story to the surface. At Muskoka Woods, we've found that one of the best early assessment tools for emerging leaders is DISC, a personal tool that groups behavioural styles into one of four dominant categories (dominance, influence, steadiness and conscientiousness) and 15 possible patterns.[4] DISC gives young people a vocabulary of self-awareness that they can take with them to any leadership situation. When emerging leaders grow quickly, it is usually because they have a particular competency that is so visibly strong that they are they get lots of responsibility in that area, sometimes too soon. Meanwhile, while one strong competency gets overused, other competencies may get ignored. Tools like DISC help give a more holistic picture that emerging leaders find very helpful.

"A leader with good character realizes their own strengths and weaknesses. And that we learned from the DISC activity with John. And learning that you have your strengths, and people realize those strengths, and that's what you want to bring to the table, but that you also have weaknesses that you need to identify in yourself. And the best way to optimize your weaknesses is to build up a team of people who have strengths in your area of weakness. So I learned that I'm a high D and a high I, which means I'm a dominate person and an enthusiastic person, but I lack attention to detail and things like that. So if I work with someone who has a high S or a high C, then they have really good attention to detail and are more focused on the behind the scenes things and getting things perfect and less on the relationships. So if the two of us are working together, we make a perfect team. Because I can build relationships and get people going, and they can be more focused on organization and detail, and that just makes us succeed so much easier and so much better."—**SUNITA**

---

[4] DISC is a personal assessment tool used by millions of people to improve teamwork, communication and performance. The tool helps identify behavioral differences and character strengths in a non-judgmental way. For more information see http://www.discprofile.com/whatisdisc.htm.

> *"Probably the DISC testing was one of the really big ones [for knowing our strengths and weaknesses] because it allowed us to just look deeper into our personalities and realize things that we might not have known."*—DEREK

As I strive to truly see young people and design effective leadership development for emerging leaders, I sometimes remind myself of the concept of magnetic variance. The true North Pole and the magnetic pole are not the same place. In fact, they are over 500 miles apart. One of the mistakes that people make in reading maps and compasses is that they fail to adjust for magnetic difference. When you are only travelling a short distance, being off by one degree doesn't make a big difference. But when you are travelling hundreds of miles, being off by one degree can make the difference between arriving at your destination and being lost in the wilderness.

When we work with emerging leaders and we don't see who they are in their inner being, we will not know how to adjust for the magnetic variance in their lives. You may set in motion the same character growth or competency sequencing or cadence exercises for every person, only to discover that those exercises have not got you to where you want to go. One of the earliest jobs in developing emerging leaders is not to paint them all with a broad brush. You need to understand what is driving them, what is their capacity to learn and, equally important, what will cause them to retreat. Each emerging leader's story is brilliantly unique.

Do you know the story of the young person that you are mentoring, coaching or seeking to serve? If you read their biography, would you be surprised? Can you describe their landscape and the way it twists and pulls them to certain postures and behaviours? Can you name their strengths? Are you open to their potential? Do you know what gives them energy? What pulls them down? Are you attentive to your own preconceptions and frames?

We often ask guests at Muskoka Woods, "What do you love about camp?" Over and over we hear "This is the only place in my life where I can really be myself." When we work with emerging leaders, one of our major tasks is to help them be free to be who they are and free to discover their best selves. This freedom grows from the fertile earth of feeling that they are seen, they are appreciated, they are valued and, most importantly, they are known and loved. When we do this, we also model for them and set a course for them to do the same to others.

Chapter 7

STRETCHING YOUNG PEOPLE TO DO AND BE MORE THAN THEY THOUGHT POSSIBLE

STRETCHING EXPERIENCES AND LEADERSHIP DEVELOPMENT

The facilitator asked someone in the class to share a story of when they were at their absolute peak performance. It was day two of the graduate course I was taking to become an executive coach. I raised my hand and stood in front of my 27 classmates. As soon as I announced I was a minister, I could see the professor visibly tense. She no doubt wondered if I was about to launch into a fiery sermon. Instead, I told the story of when I was invited by McMaster University's Divinity College to speak to preachers.

In front of my class colleagues the instructor asked me a series of questions to detail the challenge I faced. I explained that I was reluctant to accept the invitation. I felt unqualified. My first response to the invitation was, "Why do you want me? You've had all these amazing people at this event." But the organizers told me, "We don't want the big names. We want someone ordinary and accessible—someone the average person can relate to." As I continued to tell the story, the professor asked me questions to unpack

KEY MESSAGES

- Stretching experiences—challenge by choice—are the most effective way to develop leaders.

- Before you stretch the emerging leader, make sure you see the whole person and where he or she is in the sandbox.

- Effective stretching experiences need to be appropriately developmentally staged.

- Set up emerging leaders for success and stand by.

what it was about the exercise that brought me to peak performance. Eventually I said, "There's a line in the Bible where it says we mount on eagles' wings. God stirs up the nest so the baby eagle can no longer sit down. Finally, the mother eagle pushes the baby out and then sweeps under it to pick it up. Speaking at that event, it was like I was on the edge of the cliff. I've never been so stretched as that. I'm never fully alive until my wings are fully stretched."

It was a sacred moment in the room. My eyes were filled with tears, and others were too. And it wasn't because of my eloquence. It was that we all recognized the genuine truth and power of that image of the wings fully stretched, in total dependence on something bigger than ourselves.

My whole leadership development journey has been incredibly influenced by the people who created opportunities to stretch my wings—and not by the people who threw me out of the nest to let me crash and burn. To develop young leaders, we need not only to see them but also to stretch them and support them.

Cynthia McCauley is the co-editor of the *Centre for Creative Leadership Handbook on Leadership Development.* Her master's research, along with ongoing work with the Centre for Creative Leadership, has identified the three things that are most critical to leadership development: assessment, challenge and support. Assessment is about information. It shows you where you are, what your strengths are, what your needs are and how effective you are. Challenge is about experience, particularly, experience that is new or calls for skills and perspectives you don't already have. And support is married to challenge. It reassures you about your strengths and skills and builds your self-confidence.

Springing from that model, the Centre for Creative Leadership recently released some research on how leaders best learn, grow and change.[5] The research introduced a 70–20–10 rule for the value of three different types of leadership development experiences: challenging assignments (70), developmental relationships (20) and coursework and training (10). In other words, real-world challenging leadership experiences are far and away the most effective way of developing leaders.

Stretching is challenge by choice.

I can't think of a better setting to stretch young people in these real-action learning experiences than summer camp. There is probably no other place in the

[5] See Ron Rabin, *Blended Learning for Leadership: The CCL Approach,* http://www.ccl.org/Leadership/pdf/research/BlendedLearningLeadership.pdf.

world where young people can get the same opportunity to stretch their wings in leadership. In other work environments, young people often start at the bottom of the hierarchical ladder and are rarely allowed the opportunity for significant responsibility. But, at camp, young people already have deep knowledge and experience in the main subject area: fun and play. They are already experts in the field! At camp they get the opportunity to experience concrete short-term leadership challenges and get immediate feedback.

> *"Helping out in volleyball taught me that not everyone's always on the same page. There are different kids. Some were really good and had played before, but some were really terrible, and it was their first time. As a leader, we shouldn't expect everyone to have the same level of experience, so it's important to help those who are struggling."*—**KEITA**

To develop as leaders, people need stretching experiences, real-life experiences with real consequences. There are probably a handful of basic elements that most emerging leaders need to be stretched in—things like how to run a meeting, how to speak in front of a group, how to ask for help and delegate and how to be forthright and honest with people. Each of those elements can be connected to great stretching experiences.

However, beware.

Stretching experiences for leadership development involve risk for young people, and even for those who mentor and coach them. We can throw young people out of the nest at the wrong time, with the wrong task, for the wrong reasons, leaving them to crash to the ground and us to sometimes also be bruised by their fall. When we map out stretching experiences for emerging leaders, we need to make sure that we see them as whole people first, that we stage the experience appropriately and that we set them up for success (and support them when they fail).

Let's take each of these in turn.

SEEING EMERGING LEADERS FIRST

The previous chapter described the incredible importance of seeing emerging leaders for who they are and what they can become. Before giving any stretching experience to a young emerging leader, first be sure that you know where they are at. When you know a young person's story (and your own), when you see their strengths and potential (as well as their weaknesses and limitations), you are much better positioned to provide the right kinds of stretching experiences.

That first step of assessment—of really seeing young people—is often the one that gets missed. Before you give a young emerging leader a stretching challenge, ask yourself, do you know their story? Can you name their strengths? Are you tuned into their fears, wounds and disappointment? Are you in a regular rhythm of feedback with them? Do you know where they falter? Do you know their learning style? Have you checked your own judgments and frameworks and ensured that your own story is not colouring theirs? Only when we see emerging leaders first are we positioned well to stretch them.

Eagle's Flight,[6] one of the founding partners of the Muskoka Woods Leadership Studio, provides a great tool to help see an emerging leader before giving them a stretching task: the sandbox. The sandbox is bordered by four things: level of responsibility, relevant training, experience and track record.

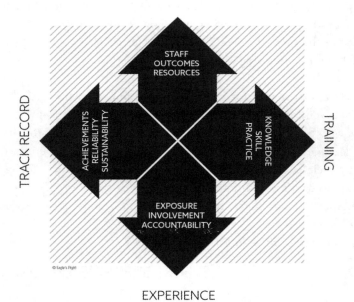

6 Eagle's Flight is an award-winning organization that provides leadership development programs through experiential action-based learning worldwide in multiple industries.

When mapping out a stretching exercise for an emerging leader, the sandbox is an image that can jumpstart you into a candid conversation. To use it, ask them, "When it comes to [this task I want you to take on], where are you in your sandbox?" They draw themselves in the box, and on a separate page you draw them in the box. Then, compare your two drawings. There may be alignment or disagreement between the two. With the drawings in front of you, you can use the differences to have a discussion and develop common understanding.

> *"When I started helping out at high ropes, there'd be little kids saying 'Oh, I don't want to do this; can I do this instead?' or 'Can I go to my cabin?' or 'Can I go lie down?' Or something. And I couldn't just say 'Oh sure, do what you want' because these are guests. I just had to put my foot down instead of being shy and reserved because I didn't want to lose the guests."*—JESSE

Knowing what is in a young person's sandbox positions a mentor, coach or sage to determine what the best kind of stretch is for this particular person, in this particular stage, for this particular issue, whether a character stretch, a competency stretch or a cadence stretch. You need to see them first.

STAGING THE RIGHT STRETCHING EXPERIENCES

I am a parent of two kids. A good parent is so attuned to the developmental stage of their child that they do not expect them to do something that is impossible for them. You don't expect a kid who has just started walking to win the Olympic marathon. Instead, skillful parents know what the right kind of stretch is for their kid. And what is an unnecessary and unreasonable expectation.

Henry Browning and Ellen Van Velsor from the Centre for Creative Leadership have some helpful vocabulary from their guidebook *Three Keys to Development*. We don't want to *underchallenge* young people, where the overlap between situational demands and current skills is so close that there is little room for growth. Nor do we want to *overchallenge* them, where there is so little overlap between situational demands and current skills that your people may become overstressed or paralyzed. Instead, we want a *developmental balance*—where there is enough, but not too much, overlap for a young person's unique stage of development.

Every year, several young people ask me if they can speak at Cadence, the weekly chapel of about 300 Muskoka Woods camp leaders. When I ask them,

"What experience do you have speaking in front of large groups?" I discover that many of them have never spoken anywhere before. If I have been able to take the time to see and know that speaking is one of their strengths, I find a way to gradually map out their development in this area. First they can speak in a cabin, then at a staff meeting, then at a larger campfire and so on. Young people will often ask me, "Don't you trust me?" And I say, "We're not having a discussion about trust; we're having a discussion about you being ready."

Part of the job of developing the leadership of young people is suggesting to them "That's not your strength at this stage." And then to say "If you want to get there, we can map out stretching opportunities for you, helping you grow that skill bit by bit. Meanwhile, let's work from where you are. The more you are able to call and collaborate with others around you, the more you will develop as a leader." This is where having an effective assessment of emerging leaders is helpful. When you know their behavioural style, you're more likely to be able to anticipate where they tend to overclaim their experience, overreach their boundaries, overestimate their capacity or overlook the risks.

The approach of leadership development that involves throwing people in deep water to see if they succeed or not often fails with young people. When young people are thrown into tasks beyond their depth, they begin to show all the early signs of immaturity—they become defensive, they resign themselves, they get paralyzed, they give up. Resist giving young people tasks that are beyond a reasonable expectation. Stretching experiences have to be developmentally staged right. Otherwise, they can leave scars from which it is very difficult to recover.

SETTING UP EMERGING LEADERS FOR SUCCESS

Anyone who has ever exercised knows the importance of stretching. I remember going out on a long bike ride. The climax of the ride was a long climb at the end. It felt fine at the time, but the next morning, I woke up and could barely walk. I had overstretched. I had pushed myself too far with too little preparation, and I was paying the price in pain. I hadn't set myself up for success. I wasn't fit enough to start, and I didn't plan my route well enough to know what I was getting into.

Older people know the danger of overstretching their muscles. For emerging leaders, overstretching can crush their spirits and cause them to flee from further leadership experiences.

92

When we set up a stretching experience for a young emerging leader, we can't set people up to fail or to lose face. If they lose trust in us, it casts a shadow over the leadership development relationship. It also may enflame insecurity and play into their fears. Then, instead of having an open disposition, they will have a disposition of fear—and you can't develop someone when they are in a position of fear. The greater the risk for failure or loss of face, the greater the risk for someone above them to also fail or lose face. Therefore, when giving a young person an assignment, measure the risk carefully. Never put a young emerging leader into a hostile environment without being prepared to also take responsibility for their actions.

When we stretch young people, how do we set them up for success?

First, when developing a young emerging leader, figure out only a small number (one or two) of essential things to stretch them on. I use a saying— "When the list is too long, something is wrong." Part of staging it right is to ensure we don't overburden the young people we are developing.

But most importantly, define carefully what the development goal is, with test marks along the way. This may be especially true for young people, who may be doing their stretching task for the first time ever. The achievement of the desired outcome is proportional to the quality of the goal. The clearer the goal, the clearer the opportunity to give the stretch.

I use CAMS to help me remember how to define the goal carefully. This framework comes from author Phil Geldart. Make sure the stretching task is the following:

C	CLEAR	Is it expressed so simply, so clearly and so precisely that the goals are truly "crystal clear" to everyone?
A	ACTIONABLE	Is it attainable, defined in actionable terms, not expressions of intent or desire?
M	MEASURABLE	Does it link quantified measurement to desired outcome?
S	SPECIFIC	Does it have a specific deadline, not a fuzzy one?

In addition to defining the stretching task well, Geldart suggests that we need to model and teach emerging leaders that there is equal onus for getting it done. Equal onus is about equal responsibility and ensuring you have what you need to do your part well. My part of equal onus is to ensure I have defined the goal carefully and done all I can to set young people up for success. Their part is to ensure they understand the goal and can get it done. If someone tells you do to something and you don't really get it, you cannot say two weeks later that you didn't really understand what he or she meant.

Equal onus is a dominant challenge when working with emerging leaders. I aim to clarify the expectations each time I give a stretching experience to a young person. Although I am not always consistent in this, when I am working at my best I use a number of questions to unpack equal onus and bring to the surface anything that might get in the way. I ask, "Are there any nagging doubts you have? Is there anything unsaid that you need to bring up? Describe to me what success looks like at the end of this. What are you going to be held accountable for? What do we do if this doesn't work?" Finally, I will also say, "In the next 48 hours, you have room to come back to me and say 'I don't understand this,' because once we commit to it, we're in this together, and I am expecting it to be done."

---

*"When we first led our WILD program, I was our selected leader, so I definitely felt a lot of responsibility. And it was a little bit stressful. The thankful part was that Jackie kept bringing up the idea of equal onus. And as a leader that makes you feel so much more comfortable. Obviously, I am still responsible, because it does have my name on it, but knowing that other people are putting their names behind it too and putting their 110 percent in makes it a lot better. That came back to me when we were leading the J2 program, because I wasn't the leader then. I was working behind the scenes. And just how easy it is, if you're not the selected leader, to just sort of slack off and goof around when the leader's not looking. But I realized that's not fair, because you're equally responsible. The fact that they're leading you means you have to also do your part. You have equal onus."—**MATT***

When young leaders do something that they really believe is right, they tend to become full of unrestrained passion, and they tend to be very idealistic—and you kind of love them for that. But, as a coach or mentor, you want to make sure that you don't allow them to go too far. Young enthusiastic leaders are prone to oversell and underdeliver. You want to make sure that their failures are not at a level that will cause them, their team or the enterprise grave cost or damage.

Much of the work of supporting emerging leaders through failure happens at the front end—you need to do the work in the beginning to not allow them to bomb. That means defining their developmental stretch as specifically as you can and telling them up front how you will evaluate the experience afterward. You cannot evaluate people on competencies they were supposed to demonstrate if you haven't identified these at the beginning.

Most mature leaders have been thrust into situations that were a big stretch for them, and as they build up experience, their resiliency for coping with those stretches grows. About a decade ago, I spoke at the Back 40 Folk Festival. The venue was a farmer's field, with the stage built into the back of a barn. My task was to give an inspirational talk right before the closing band, Thousand Foot Krutch. It was late September, dark and freezing cold. Sixteen hundred people were in the audience, and there I was, on the stage, trying to be inspirational. A kid below me in the mosh pit kept yelling repeatedly, "Liar! You're a liar!" Halfway through the talk, my voice gave out and I lost my ability to speak. I had to lower my voice to the bass register to keep going. At least two-thirds of the audience wasn't listening. They kept yelling, "Bring on Krutch! Bring on Krutch!" At the end of my talk, I walked off the stage muttering to myself, "Man, that was hard work."

A young guy was waiting in the wings, and he pulled me aside to say enthusiastically, "I want to do what you do! How do I do it?"

I said, "That's great, but make sure you have a whole lot of experience before you put yourself up on a stage in front of 1,600 people who are waiting for Thousand Foot Krutch."

If you want to see leadership grow in emerging leaders, they need to be stretched in real-life experiences with real consequences. But to be effective, those experiences have to be carefully matched with where the young leader is at in his or her own character, competence and cadence. And young leaders also need to be staged right, so that they are set up for success. Don't send the young emerging leader you are mentoring, coaching and serving onto a stage on a cold September night to speak in front of a crowd that is predisposed not to listen. Sometimes they need to be protected.

Chapter 8

SUPPORTING YOUNG PEOPLE AS THEY SUCCEED AND FAIL

SUPPORTING EMERGING LEADERS THROUGH MAELSTROMS AND CRUCIBLES

Edgar Allen Poe wrote *A Descent into the Maelstrom* in 1841. It is just as gripping now as it was then. A man recounts his tale of venturing into treacherous seas off the coast of Norway with his brother to fish. In those waters, a maelstrom—a powerful whirlpool—blows up out of a hurricane, and their boat is caught in its centre. His story of survival by letting go of the fixed ring-bolt at the foot of the mast and instead lashing himself to a barrel and throwing himself into the bottom of the maelstrom in the heart of the swirling water has a thrilling intensity.

Robert J. Thomas, who wrote *The Crucibles of Leadership: How to Learn from Experience to be a Great Leader*, uses the Poe story as a literary illustration of life and leadership. "In the clamouring rush of water," Thomas writes, "he fell into the grip of an overwhelming panic. In the moment of greatest confusion, however, with the sky narrowing above him, he was suddenly enveloped in an unearthly calm, a revelation that everything

KEY MESSAGES

- Providing support is one of the most important roles for a mentor, coach or sage.

- The more present you are, the more credibility and effectiveness you'll have.

- Young leaders will fail. Feedback and feedforward to transform crucibles into learning experiences.

was beyond his control…And in those moments of calm, he let loose his death grip on one reality and recognized another…His chance for salvation was to lash himself to a barrel and step off the ship. He did, and he survived."

For Thomas, a crucible is a defining moment, a time of trial, a transformative experience with turbulence and tension that challenges who you are. For the fisherman in the Poe story, it was being caught in the maelstrom. For a young emerging leader, it is an extreme stretching experience. Thomas argues that what matters most about these transformative experiences is how we learn from them—how we use them to mine insights and lessons for life and leadership.

As mentors, coaches and sages, our role is to support emerging leaders in the crucibles—to help them turn their stretching experiences into learning. Young leaders will have great moments of clarity and spectacular moments of failure. All across that great spectrum, young people need not only to be seen and stretched but to be supported.

THE CENTRALITY OF PRESENCE

What does it mean to support emerging leaders in their leadership development?

First and foremost it means being present with them.

Being present enables us to see them so we know them well enough to understand how to support them both personally—in their own dreams, goals, calling—and organizationally. Being present allows us to create the right kind of stretching experiences for them. And being present also means we are there to support them when they succeed and when they fail.

I learned a painful lesson about the importance of presence in the early 1990s at Muskoka Woods. I was sitting with some other senior staff by the office. On the field about 200 feet in front of me were 400 kids. A section head was dividing them into teams. He did this by calling out the kids' names one by one. You can imagine how tedious this was for the kids. After what seemed like 20 minutes, the teams were not yet even half formed, and I was growing impatient with a process that was clearly the wrong tack for the task. So I walked up to the section head and asked, "Can we do this another way and get these kids into teams and start moving?"

At that point, the program director stepped in and took control. As soon as she was finished, she walked over to where I was sitting and expressed her displeasure at my intervention.

Hers was a natural reaction. I had not earned her trust before getting involved, and that provoked a defensive response. I had not been present along the way. I had not earned permission to give uninvited direction.

I have a formula we use at Muskoka Woods that is especially true in the leadership development of young people: visibility = credibility. I've concluded that the stronger and more direct the feedback and instruction, the greater the presence you need to have had in the person's life—physically, emotionally and spiritually. If you haven't been present, good luck in having influence. And if you are not present, you cannot possibly support young people effectively in their development. There is no life change without life exchange.

Just as we need to define the way we stretch emerging leaders, so also we need to define the way we will support them. The more you define "this is what I mean by support," the better.

Will you support them,

- IN FRONT BY PAVING THE WAY? For example, there are times when I have given tasks to young emerging leaders and have quietly informed senior leaders around them, "I've asked these young leaders to step up to the plate. They probably won't deliver in the same way that you or I would. But this is worthwhile, so please help them out in whatever way you can."
- FROM BESIDE BY ACCOMPANYING THEM THOUGH THE LEADERSHIP TASK? When we walk beside, we might be on the right hand, making sure the young person doesn't overuse their strength, or on the left hand, making sure he or she has what is needed to overcome his or her weakness.
- FROM BELOW BY ALLOWING THEM TO STAND ON YOUR SHOULDERS? This is what a mother eagle does to her babies, mounting them up on her wings as they learn to fly. This is probably the most vulnerable kind of support that a mentor, coach or spiritual director can offer. Because if you lift up emerging leaders to a level that is too much for them and they fail, you will have to carry the weight of that failure on your shoulders too.

Whether you are in front, beside, below or above, supporting emerging leaders means that you are somewhere in their sphere. It takes great self-discipline to rise above being an evaluator and instead allow ourselves to enjoy the presence of emerging leaders. When it comes to support, there is nothing more important than being present. Above all, do not abandon them in their crucibles. You have to be there.

CONSISTENT SUPPORT THROUGH FEEDBACK

In my office, I often have a thick file on my desk that holds every piece of feedback I have ever received on my leadership. Performance reviews, 360-degree feedback forms, emails, reports and every tool you can imagine that has been used to evaluate my leadership style, practices and results is there. I started this file out of the deep-seated belief that I needed others to help me read my own story and to demonstrate that I take feedback seriously. Feedback reveals how other people see me and informs how I see myself.

Feedback has come up repeatedly in this book as a critical part of shaping character (since we need both self and external assessment and correction), of building competence (as a result of a learning disposition) and of nurturing cadence (as part of a disposition of openness). I've written that, along with self-awareness, feedback is the key to authenticity. As we walk with emerging leaders one of the most important ways we can see, stretch and support their leadership development is through consistent feedback. Here I want to provide some more practical strategies for giving feedback.

Over the years, I've learned some things about feedback that work well with emerging leaders. First, make feedback a regular and expected part of your mentoring, coaching or spiritual direction relationship with a young emerging leader. Giving feedback should be a regular rhythm and not an exceptional event.

Second, involve emerging leaders in the feedback experience. A friend of mine who is a vice president for a major corporation shared with me that she begins her feedback sessions with staff by saying, "Tell me three things you want to celebrate from this experience." Then she says, "If you were to repeat this, what would you do differently?" Normally, most of what the person shares echoes what the person giving feedback would have said. But, the participation and involvement of the person in the process makes the learning much more powerful.

Third, when giving feedback to emerging leaders, *don't say too much.* This is one of the most common pitfalls. Emerging leaders are easily overwhelmed by feedback in the midst of or after stretching experiences. Focus your feedback on one or two things only. This also forces you to figure out what you really want the young person to learn and grow in.

Finally, when emerging leaders come to you with big ideas, even if you know they won't work, practice PPQ—give the *positive,* explore the *possible* spinoffs to make the idea better and address your concerns by asking *questions.*

Instead of shutting them down, this approach helps emerging leaders maintain a disposition of openness to feedback.

Here's an example: I worked with a young leader at Muskoka Woods who was very ambitious and visionary in terms of programming. He came to me excited about an idea for an opening event for the beginning of camp. His idea included renting helicopters and fancy sports cars for a spectacular start to the week. I had a strong suspicion of what it would cost, how astronomical the insurance would be, what the risks were and so on. But instead of snuffing out his idea, I pointed out the positives, helped him brainstorm possible spinoffs and asked him to research the answer to some questions about insurance companies, drivers and so on. I was pretty sure I already knew the answers, but we had time and opportunity for this to be a learning moment for him. Sure enough, he came back and said, "You have to be 25 to drive the car, we don't have the budget for the insurance costs, and the idea isn't really doable." At that point I said, "OK, what else can we do?"

A regular rhythm of feedback is incredibly central to our support of emerging leaders, yet we typically wait far too long to give it. Midway through a university leadership course I was teaching, I discovered there was a teaching evaluation that I was supposed to give to my students. I was to be evaluated on criteria I didn't even know existed! Instead of waiting until the end of the course, I asked my students to take the evaluation and rate me right then on the things they wanted me to start doing, stop doing and continue doing. The most unhelpful feedback is feedback that comes too late in the process to make any difference and on criteria we weren't clear on from the start. Instead, as we see, stretch and support emerging leaders, we need to skillfully practice giving feedback to emerging leaders early and often.

FEEDFORWARD AND PROCESSING FAILURE

Feedback is fundamental to leadership development and supporting emerging leaders, but one of the most transformative things I have learned in recent years flips feedback around from back to front. The concept is called "feedforward."

Marshall Goldsmith is one of the world's preeminent thinkers and writers on leadership. Goldsmith and his colleague Jon Katzenbach coined the term "feedforward." Feedback goes in the direction you would expect—back and behind to events that have already happened and cannot be changed. Feedforward, on the other hand, focuses on a positive future rather than the mistakes of the past. So, instead of saying "This is what went wrong," the conversation is about "I want to be more effective at this. Can you give me one or two things that would help get me there?" The major switch is from looking at the past to looking at the future.

Goldsmith's article "Try Feedforward Instead of Feedback"[7] describes an exercise that can be done in partners. In preparation, each person identifies one behaviour he or she would like to change that would make a significant positive difference in his or her life. One person then expresses that behaviour change briefly and concisely to a partner. For example, "I want to be a better listener." Then, the individual asks the partner for two suggestions for the future that could help achieve that change. Suggestions should not include any feedback about past behaviour or circumstances and might begin with expressions like "I suggest" or "Here's an idea." The person who asked the question should listen attentively to these suggestions and take notes. They should not critique or comment on the suggestions in any way but should simply thank the partner for their suggestion. Then, the partners switch roles and repeat the process.

Feedforward tends to be faster and more efficient than feedback and is far less likely to be taken defensively or personally. In this exercise, there is no pressure to compose a clever reply or to try to justify past mistakes. Instead, there is only looking ahead to the future.

The concept of feedforward is particularly powerful when we are processing failure with emerging leaders. When a young emerging leader fails, it's clear to them and to you that you can't fix the past. So instead, feedforward. Call up the good stuff and feedforward on what could look different in the future. Ask them "What would you want to do differently? What could get in the way of doing that? What steps would you take to get past those challenges?" Feedforward helps span the distance between where they are now and where they want to be.

People know when they have messed up and they haven't done well. With very few exceptions, it's not a mystery to them. The goal is to have emerging leaders learn from their crucibles and turn them into active lessons for their life and leadership. The task of a coach, mentor or sage is to support them in the failure without endorsing the failure or becoming supportive of excuses or blame. Because—let's put this out there straight—emerging leaders will fail. Regularly. A teenager will get up on their skateboard and fall hundreds of times on a complicated trick before they land it. The same will be true in their life and in their leadership development.

---

[7] http://www.marshallgoldsmithlibrary.com/cim/articles_display.php?aid=110.

SUPPORTING EMERGING LEADERS TO LEARN AND GROW

When we know people's stories—including our own—one of the things we quickly discover is that we are not perfect. We are unfinished. We fail and make mistakes. As you see, stretch and support emerging leaders and build their character, competence and cadence, *do not expect or demand perfection from young people.* You will be disappointed, and they will shut down and run. One of my long-term mottos is that God loves me no matter who I am, but God loves me too much to leave me in this state. God is interested not only in who we are but also in who we are becoming.

Gordon MacDonald is a well-known Christian leader, speaker and author whom I have long admired. In his book *Rebuilding Your Broken World,* he draws from personal experience to talk about how to rebuild life in the midst of the brokenness of our world and the imperfection of our very selves. A few years ago, after a camping conference, my colleague Chris and I gave him a ride to the airport so we could ask him this question: "What would you say to us that is crucial for our leadership and spiritual development?"

His answer was wise: "First, make sure you have deep friends around you. Second, make sure you read biographies—they give you insight into what leadership is really like."

Most books about leadership as a concept are one heroic story after another. But most biographies and autobiographies of leaders are transparent, authentic and real. They help us see who leaders really are, including not only their successes and victories but also their failures and struggles. When we read biographies, it gives us permission to say "Yes, that's who I am; yes, I fail; yes, I struggle." After we dropped him off at the airport, Chris and I headed immediately to the bookstore.

When the private writings of Mother Theresa were released in 2007 in the book *Mother Teresa: Come Be My Light,* they revealed years of the absence of God's voice in a woman who has been trumpeted as one of the greatest modern-day saints. Mother Theresa's writing comforted me. The priest who compiled and presented this writing believed that it was only because Mother Theresa was in great poverty of spirit that she could relate to people in great material poverty. Her story and the stories of other leaders have had a profound impact on my spiritual and leadership development. I think it is partly because biographies remind us that we are unfinished.

Most leaders will fail and succeed. My dominant gift is speaking. There are hundreds of times I've used it to motivate people—but there are plenty of others where it has had the opposite effect. The moment that you create expectations or requirements for perfection, people will begin to pretend. We should be interested in developing leaders who are not perfect but rather authentic and real. People often say that you "learn from experience." But that's only partly true. You learn from evaluative experience. When you support people in their crucibles, you can turn them toward learning and give them the freedom to begin again.

The result of appropriate and effective support for emerging leaders is that they learn and grow—in character, in competence, in cadence, in confidence. They are encouraged, in the purest form of the word—filled with courage to act, to identify the change they want to see and to do something about it.

CONCLUSION

Over the Bridge Together

The Quebec Bridge spans the south shore of the St. Lawrence River in Lévis to its north shore in Quebec City. By 1904, construction of the bridge was underway. However, the early calculations made for the bridge's design were not checked carefully when the span was lengthened from 1,600 to 1,800 feet. As a result, the weight of the bridge was simply too heavy for its supports. By 1907, as construction continued, engineers began to notice that some of the beams were already bent. On August 29, 1907, the supervising engineer sent a telegraph to the Phoenix Bridge Company saying, "Add no more load to bridge til after due consideration of facts."

Unfortunately, the message was not received in time by the Quebec crew. That same afternoon, the bridge collapsed. Seventy-five workers were killed. Legend has it that iron from the collapsed bridge was used to forge the early iron rings worn by Canadian engineering graduates, symbolizing the gravity of their responsibility and ethics.

The Quebec Bridge collapsed because the substructure that needed to be put in place at the early stages of construction was flawed. Engineers know that if you don't have the solid substructure in place, collapse is inevitable. The same is true with leadership development. Early in the life of emerging leaders, the footings of character, competence and cadence need to be in place to support and sustain their ongoing leadership development into their twenties, thirties, forties and beyond.

Without solid character, the collapse comes when the hidden life is revealed. Then, trust is lost, credibility is damaged and influence is compromised. To grow in character, we need to be affirmed in who we are, to be authentic and to be attuned to our current reality. When we expose ourselves to feedback and the stuff we've hidden away comes out, character growth is sometimes painful. But an effective leader's character is revealed not in perfection but in authenticity.

Without competence, the collapse comes through losing face and repeated failure. All leaders fail, but without cultivating the capacity to make wise choices and deal with complexity with a learning disposition, failures will continue. Dealing constructively with failure leads to increased levels of competence for the long run.

Without cadence, the collapse comes with breakdown and burnout. When the inner life is not being nurtured, a leader is not in step with the rhythm of themselves, others and God. There is not enough strength to sustain the health of a person, their team or their organizational effectiveness. When the badge of being busy gets torn off, there is only an empty shell. We need the dispositions of openness, awareness and responsiveness to live in cadence. To continue to grow and develop, leaders need to be sustained by something bigger than themselves.

What is amazing about bridges is that with the right substructure, bridges that were built for horses and carriages in the early 20th century can now support SUVs and transport trucks. The footings have settled, but over the years they have supported increasingly heavy loads. The same goes for leadership development. With the right dispositions, principles and practices in their early years, emerging leaders will be able to tackle increasingly complex leadership challenges as they grow up into their middle life and beyond.

Over the years I have sat in many rooms with groups of people—both mature leaders and younger emerging ones—talking about how we can best equip the new generation for leadership. Some of those discussions have been provocative. Some people say that older leaders just need to get out of the way so younger leaders can step in and take over.

There needs to be room for us both.

Exceptional emerging leaders don't develop alone. They need the intention and attention of coaches, mentors and sages who walk alongside them and help them build the footings of cadence, character and competence.

Older, more seasoned leaders don't develop alone either. They too need to continually live as learners, embracing the feedback of others and the fresh ideas of young people.

Too often older leaders resist handing over power and responsibility to younger leaders. But while older leaders may cling to the reins too tightly, younger leaders have a tendency to overclaim their own capacity and disregard the wisdom and experience of others. Emerging leaders may have incredible enthusiasm and impressive competence. But when we give young people too many resources and opportunities, we risk setting them up for catastrophic failure where they lose face and lose confidence.

Emerging leaders need mentors, coaches and sages who can see them for who they are and help them unleash their best selves, who can stretch them beyond what they thought possible and support them when they succeed and when they fail. When your season as a coach, mentor or sage with young emerging leaders is done, you'll know you've been successful when they exhibit healthy self-confidence, their friendships with their teams are richer and their leadership influence is expressed with creativity and courage.

C. S. Lewis wrote in *The Magician's Nephew*, "For what a person sees and hears depends a good deal on where one is standing; it also depends on what sort of person you are." From where I am standing—looking across the bridge from the current reality to the preferred future, from the younger leader to the older, from the now to the not yet—we need each other. Leaders look at the world and say "It doesn't have to be this way" and do something about it. Let's walk over the bridge together.

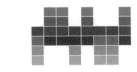